AF601782

CRYPTO INVESTING STRATEGIES FOR NON-GREEDY PEOPLE

CRYPTO INVESTING STRATEGIES FOR NON-GREEDY PEOPLE

DAVID OLARINOYE

Momentum House

First Printing, 2021

CONTENTS

INTRODUCTION

That Awkward Moment When My Money-Conservative Aunt First Bought Bitcoin

I was sitting on the sofa when I heard my phone ring. I walked back to my desk to see who was calling. The number looked familiar so I picked it up. As soon as I heard the voice, I knew who was speaking. It was my aunt. And this wasn't something that happens a lot.

Relatives don't call me very often. In fact, people don't call me often. They all know I have no affinity for idle chatter on the phone. The last time I spoke with my aunt was several months back, so I knew this call must be important. We exchanged pleasantries, and we both cut to the chase very quickly.

"How is bitcoin?" she asked. I chuckled a bit. I wasn't surprised by the question, which I get in different forms a lot, given my experience investing and writing about cryptocurrencies. This was June 2021. I had no interest in lecturing anyone about bitcoin. But all that changed when she told me she had bought some.

What the f***?

Of course, I didn't say that. And I wasn't shocked because of the fact that someone bought bitcoin. I was shocked because:

THIS WAS MY "let us buy the cheaper one" AUNT!

THIS WAS MY "I cannot put my money in what I don't understand" AUNT!

THIS WAS MY "I will not be defrauded" AUNT!

THIS WAS MY "Nobody can convince me to do a complicated business" AUNT!

I didn't really react to the news that she had bought bitcoin until our call was over. Our conversation went in a different direction, which I will get back to shortly. But when the call ended, it occurred to me that the person who convinced her to buy bitcoin at the top of the market deserved a Nobel Prize. She even said they sold her on bitcoin classes. Only God knows what they were teaching my dear aunt.

I wouldn't even dare talk to my aunt about bitcoin. And I had spent some time in her house back when I was still freshly interested in crypto. I guessed that was why she called me. She knew I knew about it somehow.

Anyway, she told me on the call that she had spent a few thousand dollars on bitcoin. And her "investment" is now down by 50% a few weeks later. At that moment, I had to reassure her that this is just how the crypto markets work.

When I gave her a suggestion on how to rearrange her strategy, she just said, "No, I am not doing this again." I chuckled. Then, I told her that if she had come to me before she made the purchase, I would have given her investment tips on how to avoid the mess her portfolio became.

Those people who say they teach bitcoin investing only teach buying and offer little or nothing when it comes to strategies for selling. I just shake my head every time I hear them. While I used to write for a top cryptocurrency publication, I got so tired of everything that I moved on in my professional life. Now I keep my knowledge to myself and just watch the circus on Twitter (from an anonymous account) for the fun of it.

I sold a significant chunk of my crypto holdings in 2020, about the time the rally started gaining momentum. Now I can afford to ignore the rest of it till the year 2098. I knew all those highs in early 2021 were the top of the market. But it was none of my business.

When we started having bitcoin conversations in my business mastermind group, I knew this must be very close to the very top. And when a real estate agent in the mastermind group sent a message to the group saying that someone was pitching him hard to buy a coin (one I had not heard of before) as it went up 20% from the day before, I knew this must be the very top. And sure enough, it was the top.

The funny thing was that I didn't know my aunt had bought into the trend too. And she was super pissed with bitcoin by the time she was on the call with me. I told her, "You should have spoken to me sooner and I would have advised you differently."

I shared with my mastermind group the story of my conversation with my aunt. Then, I realized that I had to write this book. And not just for people like my aunt. There are very few people who are totally objective about bitcoin and cryptocurrencies. On the one hand are believers (who believe bitcoin is destined to replace the US dollar, or something like that) and on the other hand are the "nocoiners," as they are fondly called (who believe bitcoin will fail and go to zero). I belong to neither of these schools of thought.

It is rare to find someone like me. So, I decided to create a strategy template:

- for objective people,
- for non-greedy people,

- for people who are tired of impulse-buying because of FOMO,
- for institutions who have yet to really understand crypto,
- for funds who don't quite understand how to class crypto in their portfolio,
- for family offices who don't want to be left out but also have yet to understand the crypto trend,
- for people who want to understand a profitable model to invest in crypto.

This is not financial advice. But I promise that there is some good stuff in here. This book was written for two reasons:

1. To get you to understand crypto investing models that are profitable;
2. To get you to laugh. Or at least smile. Or at least grin. Or at least have the thought of grinning (hence, my sense of humor).

My editor says I have to say something about myself to show I'm qualified to write this book. So, just in case you still don't understand why you should listen to me talk about the subject... Let me shill myself.

First, you have to understand that your favorite go-to person for crypto advice or insight doesn't know much (if they know anything at all). And I don't say that to brag. I see all the guys they bring on TV to talk about crypto. Even the people that talk technical stuff. And the people who have sunk millions of dollars into crypto. And if I've noticed one thing, it's that the more you know, the less you talk or care.

I got started in crypto in early 2017 and went deep pretty quickly. In a few months, I knew much more than the person who had introduced me to the industry. I was there for the bitcoin civil war that created bitcoin cash. I was right there actively trading when bitcoin hit its all-time high (at that point, at least) in December 2017. I monitored the space all through the bear market of 2018.

I started working with a crypto publication in 2018. My job was mainly to analyze cryptocurrency projects, so I did a deep-dive on a lot of cryptocurrencies. I left the publication in 2019, but I had gained a great deal of valuable insights. And I kept my interest alive by monitoring the space ever since.

I was there when Binance was just launching with their ICO. There were lots of exchanges that were launching around the same time, so I didn't really think Binance would be that special. Maybe if I had met CZ, I would have thought differently. I invested in a couple of ICOs. One was an outright scam, some failed, and I abandoned others. I invested in mining too. At some point, I joined a team that was going to do an ICO. They were planning to launch an exchange, but unfortunately couldn't raise the initial capital they needed to go ahead with the ICO.

At some point, I was an active trader. Now, I no longer consider myself an active trader. I am a fundamental analysis kind of person. And when I built my analysis (which you will see in Chapter 1) and followed it, my portfolio performed great. There was just one problem; my investment volume was too small. It was ridiculously small. I had gotten good at investing but not so good at making money. So even though I was proud of my investing thesis, it didn't make sense for me to do that full-time. So, I focused on some of my other interests and started to get good at making money.

I totally avoided talking about bitcoin and crypto until people started asking me about it again in 2021. Now, everybody is interested in it again. So, I write this book for the sake of posterity. I hope you gain something tangible from it.

The structure for this book is very simple. I will give you my thesis in the first chapter, which is an article I wrote quite some time ago and published on the internet. Then, I will spend the remaining 23 chapters defending my position and drawing out more specific strategies for different investment needs.

Let's dig in.

CHAPTER 1

A Bitcoin Investing Strategy for Non-Technical People

Bitcoin is here to stay. Love it or hate it, you can't stop it. Bitcoin doesn't care about your opinions. It is what it is.

It has been almost a year since I wrote anything about bitcoin or cryptocurrencies. Yet, people still reach out to me to give them advice about investing in bitcoin. Before I express my strategy and opinion, let me talk about my history with bitcoin.

By the way, I am not an "investment adviser" or "expert" in any way. I am just someone who has worked out a couple of things and noticed what works. This strategy is just my brainwork. You bear full responsibility for using it. I offer no promises.

But if you really think about it, I think you will find it reasonable.

THE STRATEGY (THEORY)

This strategy is based on three assumptions. Here they are:

1. Bitcoin is here to stay, and it will not go to zero. I know a couple of people who will buy all the bitcoins in existence if the price goes below $1. And if I were to get that chance, I would do the same. This is why I consider it a safe assumption that bitcoin will always have value.
2. The price of bitcoin falls and rises without much rationale. The price has wild swings. And it will continue to have wild swings.
3. Bitcoin is always readily available on the market. If you have money to buy, there is someone willing to sell.

Next, it is important to understand what bitcoin is. This is so you can understand how to class it in your investment portfolio. From what I have learned thus far about it, here are my deductions:

1. Bitcoin is not an asset. This is simply because owning it does not give you residual income.
2. Bitcoin is not a commodity. You can't use it to do anything. You can make jewelry from gold, you can get fuel from oil... you can't do anything like that with bitcoin.
3. Bitcoin has intrinsic value because miners incur energy costs to keep the network up and running.
4. Bitcoin can be used as a currency, but it is not like the currencies we are used to. The value is not backed by any government, hence it is unstable and at the mercy of the market forces of demand and supply. (El Salvador has accepted bitcoin as legal tender, but they are not backing it. No country can back bitcoin.)

There are three major ways to invest in bitcoin: mining, trading, and developing. The only reasonable way for regular people to invest in bitcoin today is by trading. However, trading profitably requires you to be emotionally aloof and disinterested. And many aren't capable of that.

The philosophy of this investing strategy is based on two concepts:

- Dollar-cost averaging
- Rebalancing

Dollar-cost averaging is when you invest the same amount every week or month regardless of what the price is. Sometimes the price will be low and sometimes it will be high, but over a long time the prices will offset each other.

Rebalancing is a technique where you take your profits when the times are very good and spread the gains on other things.

So, the strategy is to use dollar-cost averaging to buy. And use the rebalancing technique to sell.

THE STRATEGY (METHOD)

Before breaking down the method, this is just to let you know that this strategy is not for someone who wants to get rich quickly. In fact, it is not really investing. It is just a glorified way of saving money. All regular currencies of the world are constantly devaluing so they can stay competitive. So if you are saving them, you're getting thrown under the bus.

Consider investing in crypto as a way to save up your money and use it to buy assets. It is much better than saving in a bank.

It is important to know when to cash out of crypto, and then what to do with that cash.

Here is the step-by-step method:

- Download a crypto trading app that also has a crypto wallet service. It must be a platform that allows you to move money from your local currency into bitcoin seamlessly.
- Watch the fees. They are important. The platform you choose can have deposit and withdrawal fees. But make sure that they have small or no trading fees.
- You only need a platform that exchanges your local currency to bitcoin and vice versa. You don't need other cryptocurrencies (unless you are a pro). In short, don't bother your head about anything else your platform offers.
- Register on your platform and make sure you are eligible to use it. Most require some identification for proper verification. Do all that is necessary. The user interface must be comfortable and not confusing.
- Dedicate a certain amount of money from your income as the amount you will save. The percentage depends on your income size. But it must be something that doesn't harm you in the short-term. Something between 1% and 10% is reasonable. And if your income is really large, you might even do less than 1%.
- Every week or month (or however you are paid), buy an amount of bitcoin with this money, regardless of what the price of bitcoin is. You don't need to care where the price is or where it is going. Just buy that small amount.
- Stick with this gradual buying no matter what happens. In fact, don't check prices or listen to analysis. Just do this simple thing regularly
- Then set a price alert. Set a price alert for when the price of bitcoin hits a figure that will really get you excited. It could be at 50% more than when you began, or when the price doubles. But just set a high price alert.

- When bitcoin reaches and exceeds the high price alert you set for it and, of course, your money has grown quite well, then you rebalance. This means you sell half of your entire holdings
- Then you set another high price target. If it gets there or exceeds that point, you sell half again.
- You can use the half you sell to buy an asset: maybe stocks, bonds, real estate, etc. Or you could decide to enjoy yourself with the money.
- It is very important for you to sell half of your holdings when you get that surge in price. You may be tempted to hold on a little longer to see whether the price will go further up. But if you rely on such, you will be let down.
- When you sell, don't forget to keep buying according to your schedule. No matter how high or low the price, stick to your schedule.

During the short bitcoin rally in 2019, I cashed out significantly. I cashed out at $8K and then I did again at $13K. (Of course, I never sold my entire holdings.) I then used the money for something else.

Always remember that when everybody starts celebrating bitcoin in the media, it is a sign for you to rebalance. And you must be disciplined to keep buying according to your schedule, especially when they start saying bitcoin is dead (again).

This pattern has repeated itself a couple of times already. And it will happen again. Never trust your emotions. Decide what your actions will be before that time comes.

SUMMARY

This strategy is not for portfolio managers. It is for regular people with steady incomes. It is for people who have jobs that keep them busy. It is not for full-time traders or price speculators.

It is not wise to save money in the bank. If you have to save, save money in bitcoin. And be disciplined enough to sell half at the right time.

(This was first written in February 2020. And about 16 months later, there isn't much I would change about it. Now you have my thesis.)

CHAPTER 2

Reality of the Crypto Jungle

Before you start running with my crypto strategy, let me remind you that it is for bitcoin only. Using that playbook for other cryptocurrencies may result in getting rekt. ("Rekt," for those not familiar with crypto lingo, means severe losses.)

The three assumptions that make up the strategy (theory) from Chapter 1 are true for bitcoin. But they are not true of every other cryptocurrency. For most of them, they can go to zero. They can go into obscurity. And nobody really wants to hold them for a long, long time. The people who have cryptocurrencies other than bitcoin want to sell at a profit. Now, pay attention.

Say, for example, you have a friend telling you about a new crypto coin that did 200% yesterday. They are not telling you because they want you to make money. They are telling you because they are already in. And the more people get in, the more the price goes up. (It is the basic law of demand and supply.) Your friend wants to create a movement around the coin.

And there are several subtle ways to do that. One way that has gotten a lot of traction is memes. You may laugh, but they are gradually and unconsciously changing your perception. Elon Musk said it himself: "If a picture is 1,000 words, then memes are 10,000 words."

Never, ever underestimate the power of memes.

Back to the subject, other cryptocurrencies are not like bitcoin and hence should not be treated like bitcoin. Hence, the right strategy for those coins is different. I will share the strategy in another chapter. Here, I want you to see the classification of cryptocurrencies.

There is bitcoin, there is ethereum, and then there are the others. Ethereum is also in a league of its own. While I would not recommend investing in ethereum as you do in bitcoin, ethereum is more likely to give a bigger return on investment for people who want to invest millions of dollars in cryptocurrency. However, the strategy for them is not to merely buy the ether (as the ethereum coin is fondly called).

Ethereum is a platform and it has a promising future prospect. It is not perfect and it has several issues. But if one platform is going to succeed in the crypto world, it will be ethereum. It has three big qualities:

- Community
- Technology fundamentals
- Active leadership and development team

There are other platforms in the crypto space such as Tron and XTZ. But they have more obvious weaknesses. And generally their communities are not as strong as ethereum's. And in the crypto world, the community is very important. A crypto coin without a community is very likely to turn out to be a pump-and-dump scheme.

When investing in a platform coin, the questions you ask are these:

- How many apps (or decentralized applications, as they are called) are being built on this platform?
- How many of those apps are active?
- How many of those apps are not primarily funded by the platform itself?

This is how you know the strength of the community of any platform coin. And for technology fundamentals, you ask how true the cryptocurrency has stayed to its technological ideals. Whether the platform has an active leadership and development team should be obvious.

There is a case for buying and holding ether for the long-term, just like bitcoin. But the sentiment for doing so is not as strong as that of bitcoin. So you can decide to play buy-and-hold for ethereum. However, personally speaking, I don't like the idea of buying and waiting for a miracle to happen. I only recommend buying ethereum for the long-term if you are building on it. Or you are involved indirectly in building on ethereum. Otherwise, you are at the mercy of other people. And you will have no reason to keep holding on when the price is tanking.

The most important thing to consider in your crypto investment is WHEN YOU SELL. Nobody tells you this. And I see too many people make this mistake again and again. They think they are a genius for buying at the right time. And there is no right time to buy. Or, rather, every time is the right time to buy. But there is a wrong time to sell.

Most people FOMO in and FUD out. Let me break that down in simple English. FOMO means "fear of missing out." FUD means "fear, uncertainty, and doubt." So, most people buy because they don't want to miss out on the big wave that everyone is talking about. And they sell when they feel fear and see signs of doubt and uncertainty.

This means they buy high and sell low. I see this happen all the time. To be profitable, you have to sell at a significantly higher price than you buy. And so, there is a very high importance on when you sell.

So, the two areas you can go wrong in your crypto investment is:

- When you sell
- How you buy

It is not about when you buy; rather, it is about how you buy. If you are investing your personal wealth, you should never, ever buy in bulk. (More on this later).

The mistake people have with selling is that they don't have a predetermined time to sell. From the time you start buying, you should have a selling price in sight. If you don't have a sell target, I can almost guarantee that you will sell at a loss.

If FUD doesn't make you sell, you will need money. You will have an emergency. Something will come up. And you will have to dip your hands into everywhere you have money. And funny enough, those are always the times that your crypto portfolio will be in red. That's just how it happens. So, if you don't have a sell target that you stick to, you will very likely make losses.

In the next chapter, I will show you what your best friend in your crypto investment should be. Ready?

CHAPTER 3

Your Best Friend in Crypto Investing

I don't check the price of bitcoin every day. I left that foolishness behind a long time ago. So, how do I know when bitcoin is on the moon? ("On the moon" means the price is sky-high). Well, I know when people who know nothing about bitcoin (and are not otherwise interested in it) are asking me for validation to buy.

That is when I get those calls:

Hi, David, my friend was telling me about Ethereum the other day...

No matter how I try to educate people at this stage, they never listen. They just want validation. They want someone to tell them, "Yes, buy." And I will not say that. I usually push the responsibility back to them. Like I said earlier, there is no wrong time to buy.

When I start getting those calls, that's when I start looking at the price of bitcoin. And then I decide when I have had enough rally to take profits. When I took profits in 2020, my portfolio was between 3X and 5X what I had invested (I had gotten in at different times). I sold without any emotions. Bitcoin went on to double my sell price in the coming weeks. You know what? I didn't care.

This is the part where being non-greedy comes in. Trust me, I have been there. I have looked at my portfolio and known I should sell. But I kept thinking, "The price will go up a bit more." And it didn't.

The next day, bitcoin fell by double digits. I sold instantly (because I was still in profit... never sell at a loss if you can avoid it). The funny thing was that the price continued to fall that month. How can you have a fortune in crypto and go hungry in your daily life? This is the consequence of not having a strategy. Invest without planning ahead, and you'll go hungry all day and then in the evening you'll eat ramen. Not wise at all.

This brings us to your best friend in crypto investing. This is good for you whether you are investing your personal fortune, or you manage a family office, or you work as an active trader with an institution. This is good if you are investing a few hundred bucks or hundreds of millions, or somewhere in-between.

Your best friend in crypto investing is YOUR CASH POSITION. This is so underrated. Let me explain.

There are liquid assets and illiquid assets. Liquid assets are things like stocks (or "stonks," as they are fondly called in the crypto world) because you can sell almost immediately and get cash. Illiquid assets are things like real estate because it takes a while before you get cash out. Your cash position thus helps you figure out how to place those assets in your portfolio.

Now, crypto is not an asset, generally speaking. But the question here is this: is it liquid or illiquid? Naturally, crypto investing is liquid. You can sell your cryptocurrencies and get cash almost instantly. However, if you go by the strategy explained in this book, you will be treating the crypto part of your investment portfolio as illiquid.

This means you cannot take cash out any way you like. There has to be a schedule for that. Hence, to mitigate the risk of being illiquid, you need a cash position that is directly tied to your crypto holdings. This means that your crypto portfolio should look like this (ignore the specific percentage distribution, this is just to give you an idea) :

- Bitcoin - 50%
- Other cryptocurrencies - 5%
- Cash - 45%

This is 100% of your crypto holdings. This is NOT 100% of your investment portfolio (which also includes its own cash position). Your crypto portfolio must have its own cash position. This is why some people own stable coins (which are cryptocurrencies that are pegged to the US dollar 1:1). Let me give you a real-life example of why this is important.

Let us assume you are investing in bitcoin so that the investment can pay college tuition for your kids much later. It seems to make sense to just keep saving in bitcoin without any strategy or cash position. Let us assume the number you are going for is $500,000.

Let us say you hit that number in bitcoin and you don't need the money for the next 3 years. So then you get relaxed and leave the money in bitcoin. But unfortunately, the week you want to pay college tuition for your first child, bitcoin's price tanks. And the $600,000 you had suddenly becomes less than $200,000. Think about that.

The crypto market is volatile and will continue to be volatile. This is why you have to have a sell target and sell at the right time. And when you sell, you move to cash. And stay there. So, you have bitcoin (or other cryptocurrencies) for the movements. Then you have your cash position to lock in your profits.

If you don't have a cash position to lock in your profits, you are playing with fire. Your crypto portfolio must always have a cash position, and it must never be less than 10%.

Sometimes you know it is time to sell, but you don't have a need for the money. Don't leave it in crypto. Sell and hold the money in your cash position. Let it stay there. This way, you can dip into it if you have a severe emergency.

With the strategy explained in this book, you would sell maybe two or three times a year (with a bull cycle). And when the bear cycle is in full swing, you might sell once in a year, or maybe you won't sell at all. And this strategy is very good for the sake of taxes too.

The lesson here is that your cash position must never be zero. When you are investing in crypto, you must be aware that the US dollar (or the currency of your home country) is still the measure with which the pricing is determined.

Most crypto trading platforms have wallets where you can keep cash or a stable coin pegged 1:1 with cash. For the US dollar, there is USDC, USDT, and several others. Pick one you have a certain amount of confidence in. But the best option is when you can keep the actual cash, meaning that you can hold USD in a wallet.

Never forget this: your best friend in crypto investing is **your cash position**.

CHAPTER 4

The Analysis of Nonsense

This is my favorite part of crypto investing. It is the funny part.

You sit down in front of the TV. And then a journalist introduces an "expert" to the show. Then, they start discussing why the bitcoin price is going up or why it is going down. I love to watch those shows when I have time to spare. Do you know why?

Have you ever seen the meme where a guy wearing a purple outfit is sitting with a mischievous smile and the caption says, "That moment when your friend is telling you a lie but you already know the truth"? That face is my exact face when I watch crypto price analysis.

I am not saying it is all nonsense. However, most of it really is. I know you may be thinking of a few people who get TV time who know quite a lot. Trust me, everybody is a learner. Their knowledge is not much better than your guess. Bitcoin was born from the financial crisis in 2008, so it's still pretty new. There are technical experts, but there are no investing experts.

Just because a man is investing a ton of money in bitcoin doesn't mean he knows what he is doing. In most cases, those people are just gambling. And I applaud their gutsy attitude. But you know what? If you listen to their advice, you're just going to end up screwed.

Meanwhile, these heavy betters have a way of saving themselves from heavy losses.

Let me give you two cases that we can all learn from.

Here is the first. Early in the year 2021, an investor I respect, Ray Dalio, released a positive and optimistic statement about bitcoin. Several people in the crypto community became overly excited because of his words, claiming, "Ray is coming into the crypto space." And of course his company, Bridgewater Associates, manages multiple billions of dollars.

But because I have seen all these scenes before, I knew that a bear market was around the corner. And my argument is this: Ray Dalio is NOT stupid. You don't get to be one of the most successful hedge-fund managers in the world if you can't connect the dots fast. My assumption is that one of the following possibilities is true: either that Ray will get onboard with bitcoin over the next five to ten years; or that other managers in Bridgewater are already heavily invested in bitcoin, to the extent that it would have to appear on Bridgewater's balance sheet. Hence, Ray had to give bitcoin his blessing so that their investor clients are not alarmed when they receive the yearly or quarterly report.

But many people don't think. They think Ray Dalio is announcing to the world that he will buy bitcoin. But what kind of a fool would he be to announce to the world that he is planning to buy bitcoin when he knows that the price will go up immediately after his announcement.

Why did I think the bear market is near because of that? For some reason, I think Wall Street is more into shorting bitcoin than buying bitcoin. Money is financial power. Think about the balance of financial power in the world. The US dollar is not the world reserve currency by accident. There are certain structures keeping it that way. And those structures won't accept bitcoin replacing the dollar that easily. Ray Dalio is an influential personality on Wall Street. There are lots of smart people on Wall Street who can make things from his words. It is not what he says that matters. Rather, it is the attention something receives when he speaks about it. Feel free to disagree with my opinion here.

What about Jamie Dimon, CEO of JPMorgan, and his comments on bitcoin over the years? Same thing. It is not about his opinion on bitcoin. It is the fact that bitcoin gets attention whenever he speaks about it.

Here is the second case that may provide you some food for thought. This is the incident that proved to me beyond any reasonable doubt that analysis over cryptocurrency price movements is 99% garbage. In late 2017, bitcoin was crushing it. The bull run was massive. And the whole bull run was predicated on one thing: the certainty that institutional investors were coming in.

The rumors spread like wildfire. Everybody (and I include myself in this) was trying to own a piece of bitcoin before institutional investors bought heavily into it. Everybody was speaking about some "meeting" with institutional investors. The rumors built up into January 2018 before the price started to tumble. And the price tumbled hard for the rest of the year. Now, here is the lesson.

Much later in 2018, Fidelity Investments revealed that they had traded profitably in bitcoin. Meaning that when people were saying, "institutional investors were coming," they were already in. It was the retail investors, rather than the institutional investors, who were the clowns. Looking back, I think about how naive we all were to actually believe such a rumor.

I gave these two examples to tell you one thing: public information is not reliable. Everybody is playing the game. And if you don't know who the sucker is, that means it's probably you. And if you are the sucker, you should get out of the game before you get hurt. If you are going to play the crypto investing game, this is my advice to you:

Believe nothing.

It doesn't matter if someone resurrects Steve Jobs, puts him on TV, and he tells you the next price target for bitcoin; do not believe it. What you hear may be true, but I can assure you that even so there will be something wrong with it.

Be smart; have your strategy and play the game you know. News and analysis exist only to throw people who don't know what they are doing off the right path. That is its sole purpose. If you watch TV or listen to analyses advising you how to invest in crypto, you will buy wrongly and sell at the wrong time. News is garbage.

Some things never grow old. I can't count how many times China has "banned" bitcoin. In every bear cycle, there is always some bad news from China. And every analysis about the news is mostly nonsense.

This leads to a new question: is the crypto market manipulated?

CHAPTER 5

Is the Crypto Market Manipulated?

I have no proof to support an answer to this question either way. I don't have proof that shows that the crypto market is not manipulated. I also do not have any proof that shows it is. However, I have heard some high-profile rumors. And I have come to one conclusion. My conclusion is this:

It doesn't matter.

It doesn't matter if the crypto market is manipulated or not. Those who follow my strategies and recommendations will not suffer the dark fate of being manipulated by those in the know. Neither does the absence of manipulation make a difference.

In 2021, there was a famous incident that involved Elon Musk. He is known to jokingly support dogecoin on Twitter, and he gets very involved in the memes. And all those are fun. They are fun until some people start taking them seriously.

Then, those people spread their seriousness to others. And then, everybody begins to assume Elon is some kind of clairvoyant. And of course the "Elon-romance" bull run came to an abrupt end. And

I am very sure many of those people who jumped on the bandwagon didn't take profits at the right time.

Elon can do Elon-stuff on Twitter. But when he shows up in person to conversations that are or seem serious, he has to behave himself. He is the CEO of a publicly traded company. Yes, he has done some crazy things, and they have cost him in one way or another.

There is nobody in the crypto market who is looking out for you. Remember the rule from the last chapter: believe nothing. If you are one of those people who enjoys seeing that the value of your cryptocurrency portfolio has gone up since you bought in 2 minutes ago, then crypto might not be for you. The only exception here is if you are a professional day trader.

There is a saying that has become popular in the crypto space:

Buy the rumor, sell the news

This means to buy when you hear a rumor and sell when it becomes official. It sounds like great advice. However, if you are not a professional day trader (who knows what you are doing), do not follow this advice. I am yet to meet someone who is not a day trader who did "buy the rumor, sell the news" profitably. Every single person I know (who is not a professional trader) loses money on such trades every time.

ICO trades, mainnet launch, and so on have all resulted in losses. I have heard ICO pitches that sell the idea that you cannot possibly lose money by investing in their ICO. What they don't tell you is that if they run out of money for development, their 5-year projection suddenly becomes a 50-year projection.

How would you like to make 5% on your invested cash every 50 years?

Or how would you like to lose 12% on your money every year except for abnormal years when the crypto market decides to surge irrationally? This is what many people sign up for and don't know it.

The most annoying thing is when the price starts surging, some experts keep telling you about the next price target.

I had some fun during the 2021 crypto bull run. I even got into some groups where they were discussing possibilities like "Dogecoin to $1." I had a lot of fun. (Of course, I was mute throughout.) It is amazing the theories people create just to support their fantasies. And there is nothing wrong with a fantasy, but this fantasy is an unregulated global market. Plenty of things are awkward with that.

Is it that I believe dogecoin won't hit $1? Absolutely not. The price can go anywhere as far as I'm concerned. But what amuses me is the way people just build castles in the air over price targets. This is how the game is played; they have to keep the naive excited about their castles in the air while they carry away the real food and furniture.

So, is the crypto market manipulated? Honestly, I don't know. Some say the stock market is no different. I cannot comment on that because I don't know the stock market.

But this is an angle you may not see coming. The Fed and government forces can deal a severe blow to the price of cryptocurrencies. Whether you like it or not, there is a lot of institutional capital in bitcoin today. If those institutions are given a reason by the Fed and government to jump ship, they will. It may not completely crash the price of bitcoin, but it will deal it a severe blow.

One thing that does not crash bitcoin price is bans. The more various governments ban cryptocurrencies, the more people seem to want it. Therefore, if there is a drop in the price of bitcoin, it is not because China has banned bitcoin for the umpteenth time.

Stop trying to make sense of the price movements of bitcoin with news and events. There is no correlation. Whatever is happening is happening. It is not a buy signal or a sell signal. If you listen to signals like that, you will buy high and sell low. And if you think bitcoin's price has reached the lowest it can get, you are in for a surprise.

I have no affinity for day trading or reading charts. So, I find it absolutely hilarious when people start showing me charts and correlations that predict the next price target. I try hard not to laugh when it is crypto-related, especially when the person showing me the chart is not a professional day trader. But I have long since realized I can't talk people out of their excitement to make quick money.

The problem of speculating on price is not when you get wrong; the problem is when you get it right. Your first three calls were en pointe and you made money. Now you are over the moon, feeling like Richie Rich. Then, reality creeps in.

The next trade is a loss. "Oh, that was a mistake."

The following trade is a loss again. "Oh, it was a miscalculation."

Loss again. "Damn, I should have known."

Loss again. "What the f***?!?!?"

Loss again. "Let me just make this last play so that I can break even for the day."

Big loss.

Even experienced day traders have experiences like this. I once heard good advice from one of them. He said if he makes three losses in a row, he stops trading for the day or even the week. Spare yourself the trauma; don't do what day traders do if you are not a professional day trader.

So, once again, is the crypto market manipulated? It doesn't matter. Just make sure that you're not the one being manipulated.

CHAPTER 6

Don't Get Caught Swimming Naked (Altcoins)

This chapter is all about how to invest in altcoins. In case you don't understand the lingo, "altcoins" means other cryptocurrencies that aren't bitcoin. The strategy described in the first chapter was for bitcoin. Altcoins are a whole different ball game.

Before explaining the strategy for altcoins, you should know what happens during the three major market positions of crypto. We have the bull run, bear run, and flat market. The bull run is when the price is going up. The bear run is when the price is falling. The flat market is when there is no reasonable change in price.

During a bull run, money flows from regular currencies (such as USD, GBP) into bitcoin. This causes a rise in the price of bitcoin. Then, as the run continues, money flows from bitcoin into other cryptocurrencies. Due to the fact that money keeps flowing into bitcoin from the outside, the money flowing out of bitcoin into other cryptocurrencies has no negative impact on bitcoin. In fact, it is very negligible.

During a bear run, money flows out of bitcoin back into regular currencies. This creates an artificial sell-off of other cryptocurrencies. The best place to be in crypto during a bear run (aside from the stable coins) is bitcoin. As soon as bitcoin starts tanking, all other cryptocurrencies fall even lower. The only people left trading will be the day traders. Most people run to bitcoin or stable coins, or go back to cash. And some just decide to wait it out.

Now, if you own bitcoin, it makes sense to wait the bear market out. However, if you own altcoins, this is not your best choice. This is because there is no guarantee that the smaller coin you're invested in will make a comeback. Of course, crypto will bounce back eventually. But that coin might never bounce back. There are tons of examples like this.

This is the basis for the altcoin strategy. Do not use this strategy for bitcoin or ethereum. Ethereum is an altcoin, but it shows a different promise and hence another strategy makes more sense for investing in it (in my opinion). The strategy for ethereum will be explained in the next chapter.

The altcoin strategy is get-in-get-out. Altcoin trading is not the place for patience. Patience doesn't work here. Just get in (if you wish to), and get out fast. In my opinion, you should not hold an altcoin position for more than 30 days. If you are in losses on day 30 for that particular crypto coin, just sell and suck it up. The emotional damage it will do to you for holding out a bit too long will be terrible. Just sell and forget about the coin.

But 30 days is an extreme case. Normally, you should be in and out within a week. In some cases, you might even get in and out within 24 hours. That is the key to success with altcoins. If you find yourself hoping and praying while waiting, you have already been played. Just get out.

What if the coin shoots up on the 31st day? So what? This is how people who lose money in altcoin trading think. Is there a definite fundamental reason it should shoot up on the 31st day? If the answer is yes, why did you get in 30 days early? Why didn't you get in 2 days early or 1 day early? Getting in 30 days early means that you don't know what you are doing. And there is a high probability that the 31st day is going to just be like the previous 30 days.

In altcoin trading, you are there to ride the bull. Buy, watch as the price goes higher, sell. That is it. As far as I know, there is no fundamental analysis in altcoin trading. Let nobody deceive you with fancy theories. Everybody is there to make profits. The people who make money don't stay long on altcoin positions. This is another part where being non-greedy is extremely important.

First, you only trade altcoins in a crypto bull run. Unless you are a professional trader, do not trade altcoins at any other time. If the crypto market is in a bear run and an altcoin is shooting up, it is a pump (99.99% of the time). And do you know what comes after a pump? A dump. If you were not in already, don't get in during the pump. It is almost guaranteed that you will make losses.

Getting caught in a pump-and-dump scheme is like getting caught swimming naked.

A pump event usually has one or two pumps per event. And it is to catch the emotions of people. The first pump is usually a high surge that makes news. The idea is to get people talking about the coin. The second pump is to make people who got in after the first pump feel like they are smart, and to get them bragging about their gains. This will invite a crowd of noobs. Noobs are people who know very little and are innocent. They are the ones that will get taken for a ride.

In most cases, the people who got in after the first pump refuse to sell after the second pump. They believe that the price will go up again now that a lot of people are just hearing about the coin. So, in many cases, they increase their position. And then, they cry.

If you are trading altcoins, you need to know how to sell fast. Leave the long-term holding to the development team (and angel investors) of the cryptocurrency (if the cryptocurrency even still has an active development team). If you are not in some way working on the fundamentals of the cryptocurrency, you have no business holding on for a long time. Just trade and move on.

If you are not a professional trader, you will likely make losses on altcoin trades. The best gift you can give yourself is stop-loss. If you expect the price to keep going up and instead it falls by 10%, just get out. Your analysis has failed. Get out. Respect yourself and your portfolio.

Now, I know that after all my preaching here, your emotions will still bait you to do the opposite. So, hopefully after making losses a few times you will remember what I have shared here, and you will stick to the altcoin strategy for non-greedy people.

The altcoin strategy is to get in fast and get out fast, and only in a crypto bull run. Don't get caught swimming naked.

CHAPTER 7

The Strategy for Ethereum

Ethereum is a platform. It is something like Android, but for blockchain technology. They call it Web 3.0. In this classification, Android, Windows, iOS, and so on are Web 2.0. A large portion of the crypto community believes that the foundation for the new generation of the internet age is going to be founded on the blockchain (which is the technology on which cryptocurrencies are based).

This leads to the assumption that there must be an operating system for blockchain applications (or decentralized applications, as they are fondly called). And ethereum is leading in this respect. There are other platforms, but, as described earlier, none is as strong as ethereum at this moment.

So, the long-term play for ethereum is that the online world will move to decentralized applications sometime in the future. And the majority of those apps will be built on ethereum. But this is an assumption. There is no certainty as to when or whether it will happen.

So, here are the strategies. The first is to invest in a team that is building an app on ethereum with a clear timeline of profitability. Now, over 90% of apps built on regular platforms such as Android, iOS, etc., do not make any money. So, what is the chance of an app on ethereum making money? You have to think about that as an investor.

The way I propose to go about this is to have a company that is like an incubator. The company should have a few ventures that are already profitable ventures (perhaps, outside of crypto). Invest in a couple of app ideas on ethereum (and be flexible to dump ideas that didn't take off after a reasonable timeline). Then, buy and hold a good amount of the ethereum coin.

The buying strategy will be to buy in batches, and only in a bear cycle. In a bull cycle, use the ethereum coins for valuation, and use it to get more cash from banks and financial institutions. The idea is to never sell ether until Web 3.0 gets mainstream adoption.

This strategy is a play for investors with millions of dollars to invest in crypto. And of course there are several investment companies today that are focused only on crypto. And the best ones (who know what they are doing) are investing in projects that are building the infrastructure for the mainstream adoption of Web 3.0. And hence, they don't care much about the bull and bear cycles.

There are other investment companies that are not solely focused on crypto, but they have a few crypto projects in their list of investments. The principle is still the same. At this stage, finding a profitable project in the crypto space is hard. And thus, it is better to fund an infrastructure project.

If you run an investment fund and you want to get into the crypto world, first seek help from an honest crypto-veteran who understands the space. You will need to draw up a strategy that will inform your choices. Making decisions off the top of your head in the heat of the moment is a very bad idea.

For everyday people, if you are developing on ethereum or your work is connected to that and you believe in what you are doing, you can do the buy-and-hold strategy. It will give you the confidence to pitch what you are doing to anyone. Also, if you are developing on any other platform coin and you believe in what you are doing, you can buy and hold that crypto coin.

But if you are not a developer and you are not a long-term investor with millions of dollars, refer to the altcoin strategy in Chapter 6.

If you are a believer in ethereum as opposed to bitcoin, then you can go with the strategy in Chapter 1. But don't say I didn't warn you. Yes, ethereum is here to stay, but there are many things that can go sideways with Web 3.0. There is no certainty that ethereum will realize its future potential. Bitcoin, on the other hand, doesn't need future potential. The present realization of bitcoin is enough to carry it for the next 100 years and beyond.

CHAPTER 8

The Madness of the ICO

The biggest misconception people have about the ICO is that they think it is like an IPO. They are two very different concepts and events.

ICO means Initial Coin Offering.

IPO means Initial Public Offering.

Both are used to raise money from the public. This is where the similarities end. If you think you have a deep understanding of IPOs and you want to apply that knowledge to ICOs, you will lose money.

An IPO is a highly regulated event. Companies prepare for an IPO as much as five years in advance. There are certain thresholds, landmarks, and milestones a company is expected to reach before attempting an IPO.

An ICO is raising money from the public through a system and method that didn't exist prior to 2008. Even though there are some regulations surrounding ICOs today, I doubt that the institutions who created those regulations fully understand what they are dealing with. And this means a lot of bad eggs will find loopholes, and a lot of good eggs will never get the chance to get off the ground.

An ICO is how many crypto projects get started. Whereas companies hold an IPO at a later stage of growth. Companies do not launch with an IPO.

People invest in an IPO fundamentally because they have seen what the company has done and what they are capable of doing. But investing in an ICO is entirely based on promise. You have not seen anything they have done. It is all about what they are going to do. And that can be very dicey.

People get to own part of the company when they invest during a company's IPO. Meanwhile, you do not own any part of the company or project when you invest in an ICO. Owning coins is not the same thing as owning shares.

When you own shares in a company, if anything goes wrong, the assets of the company can be sold to pay the shareholders. If you own coins and something goes wrong, the assets of the company or project that issued the coins to you are off-limits. You cannot have them sell their assets to give you your money back.

The coin is a commodity or currency in the ecosystem of the project that created the coin. And therefore, you are paying to participate in that ecosystem when you buy the coins. This is like a company selling loyalty cards to customers. Or it is like selling (future) coupons to customers to raise money.

Therefore, if you have no skill, interest, or desire in participating in the ecosystem of a crypto project, it seems senseless to buy into their ICO. That is, unless you are planning to buy now (on the cheap) and sell to their customers (or people who will use the crypto ecosystem) in the future (at an increased value). And this makes some kind of sense, until...

Until you realize that the crypto project has no future.

An IPO turns a privately owned company into a publicly owned company. An ICO launches an ecosystem of some kind of trade and transaction. If you are going to be using that ecosystem, then you are right to invest in the ICO.

Before holding an IPO, a company would have had to prove that it is a good steward of money. There are lots of smart people that read public financial statements and can find out any discrepancies. After the IPO, the company will have to be public about what it does with the money raised.

A crypto project is under no obligation to disclose how they spent the money they raised from ICO. They don't even have to show any proof of good financial stewardship beforehand. Even if they mislead people, they cannot be punished by market forces. The only repercussions they may suffer are lawsuits if the ICO turns out to be an outright fraud.

In summary, there are no checks and balances for an ICO. But it is not a Ponzi scheme. The technological infrastructure for crypto projects makes the promise of returns on your investment plausible. However, if the cryptocurrency in question has no technological infrastructure, then it may be likened to a Ponzi scheme in that the founders are raising money primarily for the sake of raising money, and nothing more.

The development and maturity of IPOs and the stock market took decades. The crypto world is more complicated, hence it will take a while before we have a good financial structure around ICOs. So in the meantime, investing in ICOs is for technical people and not regular people.

If you are new to crypto or you don't know much, stay away from ICOs. The only exception is if you are trying to support the project of your friend, or if you are a technical analysis person with a strategy.

If you run an investment fund or you have millions to invest in crypto, buy the team, not the coins. You can own a decent amount of coins if you already own the team. The project may be hard to own (because it should be decentralized). A good team will always come up with solutions. However, due to their decentralized nature, most crypto projects lack a financial "adult" that is responsible for the team. This is why many projects have stalled, forked, and failed.

You need a certain level of sophistication (or madness) to participate in an ICO. If you have neither of the two, stay away.

CHAPTER 9

Signs of the Top of the Market

Is there a way to know if the bull run is in full swing and the market is right at the top? Yes, there is. But the first thing I will tell you is to go back to Chapter 1 and just follow the strategy. If you follow the strategy, you don't need to know the top of the market.

Most people who really want to know the top of the market will be in denial when the top actually comes. This is because it won't be common sense to sell at that time. And this is another place where it's important to stay non-greedy.

You don't need to know the top of the market so that you can sell. Knowing the top of the market just makes you someone who can give a good, casual piece of advice. And the more people we have in the world like that, the better.

There are 11 signs that the crypto market has reached the top. This doesn't mean it can't go up more. It just means that a bear cycle is nearby. I have seen this happen three times in recent years:

- Late 2017/early 2018

- Mid-2019
- Early 2021

So, here we go.

FIRST SIGN: A NEW BITCOIN OR CRYPTO BULL IS GETTING FEATURED IN TOP TV STATIONS

A bitcoin or crypto bull is someone who believes in the prospect of bitcoin and/or cryptocurrencies as opposed to fiat currencies (such as US dollar, euro), stocks, bonds, commodities, etc. There is nothing wrong with someone being that way. But when they are getting airtime on several top TV stations, it's a sure sign the top of the market is close.

If it is a regular contributor of the TV station, that doesn't count. The person has to be someone new to the mass accumulation of bitcoin. Maybe someone who has been an investor but previously has been indifferent or opposed to bitcoin.

When you hear people everywhere saying, "I am buying bitcoins in large quantities and this is the historically correct thing to do," the top is close. There are several people who have fallen into this category of vocal bitcoin bulls. The funny thing is that they move quietly in the next bull market. This is because they finally get the game.

There is always a big investor in bitcoin or crypto who is going to be loud in the bull market. When they start getting the attention of the major TV networks, the end of the bull run is near.

SECOND SIGN: "MONEY-CONSERVATIVE" PEOPLE WHO KNOW NOTHING ABOUT BITCOIN WANT TO BUY AND LEARN

These are people like my aunt (in the introduction). When people like this start calling me and asking me about bitcoin, I know the end of the bull run is near.

When people who have zero affinity for things like crypto start telling you they bought some bitcoin, the end of the bull run is near.

THIRD SIGN: RICH PEOPLE START GETTING PITCHED A (PREVIOUSLY UNKNOWN) CRYPTOCURRENCY

I knew for sure that the market was at the top when a high-end realtor in my mastermind group shared that someone was pitching him to buy a cryptocurrency that I had not heard of before (that probably didn't exist two years ago).

FOURTH SIGN: THE BITCOIN OR CRYPTO COMMUNITY ON TWITTER ADOPTS A NEW MEME THAT CAN BE SHOWN WITH THEIR DISPLAY PICTURE

Once upon a time, it was the bitcoin sign in their eyeballs in the picture. Of course, it would start with one person and then go viral. The sign is not the meme or picture edit itself. Instead, it is when everybody in the community is doing it.

In 2021, it was laser eyes. The laser eyes feature is cool, don't get me wrong. But when you find everybody just changing to that and it is trending on Twitter, a bear run is around the corner.

FIFTH SIGN: THE BITCOIN BEARS HAVE BEEN AWKWARDLY SILENT FOR A WHILE (OR HAVE CHANGED THEIR MINDS)

There are people who don't think favorably about bitcoin. Some think it is illegitimate. Some think it is a new kind of pyramid scheme. And they are always vocal about their antagonism. When you see someone who is usually very vocal about their disgust for crypto or bitcoin become silent for too long, then "happily forever after" is about to end.

The crypto industry needs naysayers. When they have gone silent for too long and the bull-believers are everywhere singing the praise of crypto, bear runs seem to always be right around the corner.

SIXTH SIGN: WHEN THE BULL RUN HAS GOTTEN THE ATTENTION OF THE CENTRAL BANK

When you have journalists pressing the Fed Chairman (in the US) to comment on bitcoin during an impressive bull run, that is a strong sign. It is like taking a stick and poking the sleeping bear. The bear doesn't happen immediately though. It often takes effect a few weeks afterward.

Most people in the crypto community view crypto as an alternative to the traditional financial system. And the reality of money flow is still determined by the traditional system. So, if you ask them to prove if they are still in charge, they will prove it. It just takes one policy or one regulation to bring in a new bear run.

SEVENTH SIGN: WHEN THE OPPOSITE OF WHAT CAUSED BIG INVESTORS TO RUN TO CRYPTO IS HAPPENING

In 2020, a lot of investors ventured into crypto because the majority of economic activities in the world were shut down. So, many investments underperformed (even though the central banks kept printing money to avoid a global bankruptcy).

In mid-2021, economic activities started to open up. And hence, money began flowing back into the street from wherever it was held up. Crypto was one of the places money found a place to hide. And when the money started going back into the street, this meant investors were selling their bitcoin to put their cash back to work.

EIGHTH SIGN: WHEN "BITCOIN" OR "BITCOIN PRICE" HIT AN ALL-TIME HIGH IN GOOGLE SEARCH TRENDS

When a lot of people (more than normal) are searching what the price of bitcoin is on a daily basis, it means the market is flush with people who are gambling (and not investing). This means it is a good time for the people who know what they are doing to take profits.

NINTH SIGN: WHEN US SENATORS (WHO KNOW NOTHING ABOUT BITCOIN) START TALKING ABOUT IT

It doesn't matter whether the talk is positive or negative. A conversation about bitcoin on Capitol Hill is not a good sign. It may be a good sign for the long-term if they are talking in favorable terms towards bitcoin. But it is a bad sign for the short-term that they are talking at all about it.

Say, for example, Uncle Joe who knows his nephew has made a fortune on bitcoin hears his favorite senator talk about bitcoin. This will then trigger an action response from Uncle Joe. Whatever that action is, it is a bad sign for the bull run.

If Uncle Joe asks his nephew to help him buy some bitcoin, it is not a good sign. If Uncle Joe tells his nephew to get out of bitcoin, it is not a good sign. It's not the action itself that is important, more so the fact that Uncle Joe is getting involved in bitcoin at all while knowing nothing about it.

Crypto influencers keep making a key mistake. The goal is not to get everybody to buy (or own) bitcoin. Instead, the goal is to get people educated about bitcoin. You want people taking action after they are educated, not after they see their neighbor make an extra $20K from bitcoin.

TENTH SIGN: WHEN CRYPTO EXCHANGES YOU HAVE FORGOTTEN YOU OPENED AN ACCOUNT WITH START SENDING YOU FREQUENT EMAILS

Nobody sends you an email saying, "Hey, bitcoin is down 12% from yesterday, come trade your hard-earned cash for bitcoin because it has a great future." The crypto exchanges send emails when the price is up and going up sustainably. They send emails when they know you must have heard about Jenny down the street (who is not as smart as you are with money) making $10K from crypto yesterday.

And the emotional pitch always works. It will still work on some people who are reading this right now. No problem if they still get you. Just make sure that you have the strategy from Chapter 1 working for you regardless.

ELEVENTH SIGN: WHEN YOU START CALCULATING HOW MUCH YOU WOULD HAVE MADE IF YOU HAD EMPTIED YOUR RETIREMENT FUND AND PUT EVERYTHING IN CRYPTO

When you start feeling this way, you can be sure there are other people feeling that way too. And some people will actually make calls similar to this at this time. The problem is not the fact that you start buying bitcoin. Instead, the problem is this simple question:

Will you have the cash when you need it?

One day, you will need cash badly. If you have to sell your cryptocurrencies that day, you have not been smart with your crypto investment. And if you think you can one day become a billionaire by buying enough bitcoin, the next chapter is for you.

CHAPTER 10

How To Be a Crypto Billionaire

I have good news and bad news here. First, the bad news; If you are just learning about crypto, you are late to the party to becoming a crypto billionaire. Now, the good news; you can still get insanely rich from crypto.

If you want to be a crypto billionaire, you have to be a leader in the space like CZ (CEO of Binance), Vitalik Buterin (co-founder of Ethereum), or Brian Armstrong (CEO of Coinbase). You must create a company that will become an important bedrock in the crypto industry. You don't buy coins to become a billionaire.

And if you want to be a billionaire, it is almost too late to advise you to create your own cryptocurrency. The industry is tired of that, unless you have very strong fundamentals. Your cryptocurrency will just be mundane.

Creating a crypto project is like starting a political movement. If your crypto project lacks momentum (meaning that it is not worth an evening discussion among elites and everyday people), it will just be one of the many cryptocurrencies with no significant traction.

If you say you want to create your own exchange, can you compete with the top exchanges on the market? You can claim your app is better, but would anyone agree with you? Would anyone even care? Why should people leave their exchange and come to yours? And there are tons of good crypto exchanges.

However, there is a plot twist that can make anyone a billionaire. But it will be hard to pull off. And that is to acquire an exchange and merge three or four crypto exchanges to create a powerful crypto exchange. Good luck to having those exchanges agree to merge, though.

The other option is to develop a crypto project on a platform like ethereum. But building a project on ethereum will make those who have invested in ether rich before it makes you rich. And your project will always be behind ethereum. Most projects developed on Ethereum thus far are other platforms that are trying to compete with Ethereum in the long-term. There are other interesting projects coming up, but how successful they will ultimately be is only a guess.

The most plausible way of becoming a billionaire is to create a kind of hedge fund that manages other people's money. That comes with a lot of risk. It seems to be a method that will never go out of style. But you have to know what you are doing and deliver.

You may be thinking you can do this with the strategy explained in Chapter 1. But I will stop you right there. When you are managing huge funds, the strategy in Chapter 1 is no longer applicable. This is because your trades have the tendency to move the market. And so, you have to play smarter. There are other strategies for large investors. And they have very little to do with buying and selling. Unfortunately, this can only be properly explored and explained in a private consulting setting.

It is easier for someone who is a multi-millionaire already to become a billionaire with crypto. Anyone who is committed to building something incredible on crypto will have to satisfy themselves with being a millionaire. It might take some time, though.

That said, I will strongly advise you not to consciously dwell on your goal of becoming a millionaire or billionaire by investing in crypto. If you do, you are liable to make mistakes because of your emotions. The moment your emotions become a dominant factor in your investment choices, you are very likely to make losses.

Let your goals be connected to what you want to do with your money rather than how much money you want to have or make. And let's talk about emotions.

CHAPTER 11

Deleting Your Emotions

When it comes to crypto investing, don't bring your emotions. Leave them with your family and friends. And I really mean this, even though I know that many won't listen. If you get emotional about crypto, you will make mistakes.

There are people who believe in leaving civilization to live in the woods. They believe that civilization will soon crumble and they'll have enough bitcoins to start over. Well, I am not saying this civilization won't crumble. But is it reasonable to throw away all the conveniences this civilization has brought us?

Nobody knows the timeline of anything, so why not just enjoy your life the best way you can today? If living in the woods alone is your definition of enjoyment, then go for it. But if you are like me and you love penthouse suites, go for it.

The point of this chapter is that bitcoin is not life. Cryptocurrency is not life. Life is life. Bitcoin is bitcoin. Live your best life every day. Put your emotions into living your life. If bitcoin crossing an all-time high is going to make you walk with an extra spring in your step, you are in trouble. That fake joy will soon turn into sadness.

And I see this all the time on Twitter. During the bull run, you see tweets like, "Those who doubt the value of bitcoin are like the trained typewriter operators of the 1980s. They know their time is coming to an end."

The bear market comes and the narrative shifts: "Bitcoin is still the best-performing asset of the last 10 years." The problem is not whether those statements are true or false. The problem is the state of mind of those who say and hear such things.

On the day I am writing these very words, I checked my crypto wallet for the price of bitcoin after several weeks. The charade has been quiet for some time. So, I wanted to know what was going on. The price chart would tell me the story, without frills. The chart never lies.

How does one know when to sell if they never check? You set a price alert. Or if you are paying attention to wider discussions, you should check when people start bragging about crypto. And don't join them in the bragging. Here is the big secret of the crypto industry:

Amateurs talk about the future.

Experts talk about the past.

Legends laugh at the experts and amateurs.

Do you know who the suckers of the game are? They are the ones who get excited about the price of bitcoin.

Think about this when you are having a conversation with people about bitcoin. Who is the amateur, who is the expert, who is the legend, and who is the sucker of the game? It is not hard to figure out.

In crypto conversations, listen carefully. If you're talking with suckers and amateurs, change the subject. Talk about butterflies or cars. If there is an expert controlling the conversation, you can ask questions just to feed your curiosity. If a legend is in the conversation, watch their reactions to the discussion.

And don't take anything too seriously. Experts do create narratives to fit their ideas. Amateurs are often excited about what is not in their control. Why do the legends laugh? They see the lies.

Deleting your emotions doesn't mean you can't laugh and have fun in discussions. Deleting your emotions is in the context of your investment. You can be emotional about everything as long as it is not your crypto investment. When you look at the new value of your crypto holdings and you can't help but smile at how high it's gone, you should sell. Don't be greedy. Sell. Exit when the joy hits. But never completely empty your crypto holdings.

If you are smiling at the amount of money you have in bitcoin (as a result of a higher price), it means that amount means a lot to you. And you will probably be very sad if it goes down.

This is how to delete your emotions. If you want to be very effective at this, you can let your partner (who is uninterested in crypto) read this chapter. So, when you are in denial about how excited you're getting about your crypto holdings, they can be honest with you: "Honey, you are smiling at the new price of bitcoin."

Or you can get your kids involved if they have a natural interest in crypto. Don't let them make your investments. Instead, allow them to track it. When they get excited and you can't help but get excited too, that is a good time to sell (just in case you set an outrageous price target).

CHAPTER 12

NFTs

NFT is an acronym for "non-fungible token." This is a very important concept, which can be easily explained in the context of the art industry.

A painting by a famous painter (who has been dead for decades) goes up for sale in an auction. How do they know that the painting is original and not counterfeit? The industry has its processes. Once it is verified as the original, the painting can sell for millions of dollars. But digital art doesn't have the same process.

Digital art has been of low value because there is no way to determine originality. Meaning that if someone copies a work of digital art, there is no way to tell the original from the copy. And many copies can be made. This gives the art little or no value. But NFTs change that.

By turning artwork into an NFT, you create an original copy that can be verified on the blockchain. A blockchain is a type of digital ledger that records transactions and saves them on multiple computers distributed around the world, making it close to impossible to alter any transaction. To do so, you would have to hack thousands

to the NFT you own. Or when you get an offer you cannot refuse. And if you are a collector with no intention of ever selling, just make sure someone else can access your NFT collection in case something happens to you.

CHAPTER 13

Bitcoin ETFs

This chapter is for investors that are quite sophisticated and know what they are doing. If you have no idea what an ETF is, then the ideas in this chapter are not for you. But for the sake of adding to your knowledge, you can skim along.

ETF is short for "Exchange Traded Fund." And this has nothing to do with crypto. This deals with the stock exchange. There are several ways to invest in the stock exchange. You could buy stock in a company, such as Apple. But then, your investment is only limited to Apple. If anything happens to the stock price of Apple, your investment feels the direct impact.

You could also buy a mutual fund, which comprises many stocks. For example, a tech mutual fund would have stock of companies like Apple, Microsoft, Google (Alphabet), etc. So, when the price of one is down, your portfolio doesn't feel much impact because of the other stocks that are included in the fund. But mutual funds have some problems. The major ones are that they have significant broker fees, and they are only traded at the end of the day when the market closes.

So, enter the ETF. An ETF can consist of stocks, bonds, and commodities all in one basket. And they can be easily traded on the stock exchange at a price determined by demand and supply. The broker fees are less significant, they are more liquid, and they can be traded as swiftly and easily as a stock on the exchange. No need to wait for the end of the day like the mutual fund.

There are lots of ETFs. And new ones are being created. And so, there is a bitcoin ETF. Why a bitcoin ETF?

You can only trade bitcoin and other cryptocurrencies on a crypto exchange. Some people prefer to trade it on the stock exchange market. So, the bitcoin ETF was created to mimic the price of bitcoin on the stock exchange.

If you buy a bitcoin ETF, is that the same as buying bitcoin? Hell no. The ETF is for stock traders to trade bitcoin on the exchange. It is not to own bitcoin. And I have a sneaky little feeling that its real purpose is to give Wall Street the chance to short bitcoin. This is because you can't short bitcoin on crypto exchanges. You can only buy and sell.

So, two questions. First, who should buy (or trade) a bitcoin ETF? Someone who is a pro at trading securities on the stock exchange. This is only for people who know what they are doing.

And second: why would anyone want to short bitcoin? I think the answer lies in a common saying among Wall Street traders that "the bull climbs up the stairs while the bear jumps out the window." This means when the price goes up, it goes up gradually. When the price is going down, it tanks fast.

If you are a sophisticated investor that wants to make money in every bitcoin cycle, then you would need a bitcoin ETF to open up short positions for the price crash. The existence of bitcoin ETFs now means that bitcoin's price can have sharper and more volatile bear runs.

For people, institutions, and family offices investing millions of dollars into the crypto industry, you should make a bitcoin ETF (or more broadly, a crypto ETF) a part of your investment portfolio.

On the other hand, if your crypto investment portfolio is below $1 million, there isn't any reason to have a bitcoin or crypto ETF in your portfolio. That's just my opinion, though. If you try to play a game you don't understand, you will get burned.

CHAPTER 14

The Sharingans a.k.a. Taxes

I am not about to give you tax advice. That is the job of your CPA. Instead, I am here to make you aware that in all your investment dealings, keep it at the back of your mind that you will have to pay taxes on trades.

If you think dealing in cryptocurrencies is a way to escape taxes, you are dead wrong. There are tax regulations that pertain to cryptocurrencies in most countries. You should seek tax advice from your CPA as you flesh out your strategy.

This is very important if you manage a pretty hefty portfolio. You don't want to implement a strategy successfully and be impressed with yourself only to find out that you will pay back all the gains in taxes.

This is another reason why the strategy in Chapter 1 makes a lot of sense. Selling crypto at a profit is a taxable event in most countries (and cases). So, if you sell 157 times throughout the year, you'll probably be taxed 157 times (on your gains in the local currency, not on your crypto). Meanwhile, the price of every cryptocurrency is volatile.

The lesson here is not to put yourself in a position where you have to go find money to pay the taxes you owe the government. Understand how taxes work in your country with regard to cryptocurrencies. Then, adjust your strategy based on that.

Trading crypto without understanding how they will be taxed is like flying an airplane without knowing how to land. The big problem is that you think you are a genius all the way while flying, and you are oblivious to the sharingans (i.e. problems) waiting for you at your destination.

Learn how to land an airplane before you get it in the air. It is not "profit" if it all goes back into the government's purse. Talk to your CPA today.

Keep in mind that there are also certain tax advantages associated with trading bitcoin. First, the laws don't consider bitcoin a security. This means that the laws that affect stocks and bonds don't affect bitcoin. Bitcoin is considered a property, much like real estate. This means you can capture your losses and use them to your advantage when dealing in taxes.

I won't talk too much about that. Do speak to your CPA. There are two investing models to evaluate investments in this context (which I learned from Sharran Srivatsaa of Srilo Ventures). The first investing model is known as the parking LOT, where:

L stands for Liquidity

O stands for Ownership

T stands for Terms

Liquidity means how fast you can turn your investment back into cash. Bitcoin scores very high with liquidity because you can go to any exchange and sell your bitcoin for cash in a matter of minutes.

Ownership means that you have the rights to the assets as your own. If you buy bitcoin from crypto exchanges, you do have that. But if you buy a bitcoin ETF, you do not have that.

Terms means that the rules you have to follow for the investment are favorable to you. The terms of your bitcoin investment depends on your strategy.

Defining an investment with this parking LOT model can help you understand the investment. And now that you understand the investment, you have to make a decision on whether to invest or not. This introduces the second model, which is divided into four categories:

- Capital Preservation
- Equity growth
- Yield
- Tax advantages

Capital preservation means that your capital is secured. It means you are not at risk of losing the capital you invested. Bitcoin clearly doesn't have that. You are always at risk of losing your capital.

Equity growth means that your invested capital will grow in value. Yes, bitcoin has this. However, the price is volatile. And this means your gains depend on when you sell.

Yield means that the investment produces passive income that is apart from the capital. Bitcoin doesn't do that unless you go stake it to earn passive income. There are several opportunities around staking bitcoin, but you should always read the fine print. There are other cryptocurrencies that have staking built into their model, but the price volatility of crypto can make things go wrong.

Tax advantages mean that the tax laws of your country allow you not to pay tax on certain conditions when trading. For example, I heard a rumor that if you are in America and trade bitcoin from your

IRA, you won't have to pay taxes on your gains. You would have to confirm this from your CPA though.

If you can find a way to improve and answer YES to these four categories, that would be very good. But you must also think about the risks associated with your investment that could get in the way of following through with these benefits.

This is a framework to understand an investment, not financial advice. And I shared this because it brings taxes into the mix. You must think about your taxes in your crypto strategy. Don't fly an airplane without knowing how to land.

CHAPTER 15

The Three Wise Moves

There are three unorthodox ways of making money from crypto that I want to share here. I consider them unorthodox because they don't have anything to do with crypto directly. Rather, it is all about taking advantage of the trend.

The first wise move is to fund a crypto brand. As of writing, this is still uncommon. But it will become increasingly common as the crypto industry matures. Let me explain.

Generally, crypto has a problem when it comes to mainstream adoption. That will remain a problem for a while because people don't really understand how to class cryptocurrencies. Crypto will ultimately break into the mainstream through brands, and especially personal brands. It is when a platform is created for people who have a deep understanding of crypto (and can break it down for regular people) that true mainstream adoption kicks in.

By mainstream adoption, I don't mean everybody buying crypto. Instead, mainstream adoption means cryptocurrencies becoming routine in people's lifestyles. There is still a lot of FOMO and FUD about crypto.

Financially backing a brand that fosters this kind of adoption would be very beneficial. However, the details of the business structure would have to be fleshed out before getting started. But this move allows money to flow into crypto from local currencies. People want to listen to a trusted brand or expert or authority on a subject. Being that brand will open the door to a lot of other opportunities for you.

The idea with this first move is to financially back a brand (especially an organization brand) that is going in this direction. It is a cool way to make money in crypto without actually buying any crypto.

The second wise move is to create an educational program or institution about crypto. This is different from the first move, where you are in the shadows backing a brand (which can be a person, an institution, a group, etc.). By creating an educational program, you are putting yourself in the spotlight.

There are tons of educational platforms like this both online and offline. So, merely creating one is not the wise move. The wise move is to create one with perpetual clients, and ideally you will have the clients before you start out. If you start out and then start looking for clients (who will keep requesting your services), then the move is not so smart.

The idea here is to position before you begin. And you want clients who will keep sending people to you. For example, if you create an arrangement with a business school or college for your educational platform to handle crypto-related courses, that is a good vantage point.

The third wise move is to have your own media channel. It could be having your own TV channel to talk crypto. Yes, there are tons of podcasts, YouTube shows, and even TV programs that talk about crypto. This is not about creating another one. This is about creating a big media channel to be ahead. Think about the way Bloomberg TV has dominated the stock market media coverage.

However, due to the unregulated nature of lots of activities in the crypto space, a media channel to talk about trades will be misunderstood. So, the channel has to stay away from talking directly about trades and just focus instead on the development of the industry.

The crypto industry has some high rollers already, so a successful media channel like this has to gain the respect of the big names in the crypto industry without falling into a faction. It must be a worthy referee of the crypto industry, and it must also gain the trust of the non-crypto business world.

There is no respected, trusted referee of the crypto industry (from a media standpoint) as of this moment of writing. The first media platform that proves itself to be trustworthy and reputable with regards to reporting on crypto will make a fortune. In fact, they will be able to set a new standard in journalism for mainstream media.

In summary, there are three wise moves with the potential for making good money in crypto without actually trading crypto:

1. Financially back or partner with a brand that is fostering better mainstream adoption (and share from the business opportunities);
2. Create your own educational platform with recurring clients;
3. Create a media channel that wins the respect of stakeholders in crypto and business people outside of crypto.

But there is one catch to these three moves. The deal you make is only as good as the people you are dealing with. Pick your business partners wisely.

CHAPTER 16

Fake Teachers

This book is not about teaching you the fundamentals of cryptocurrency, blockchain technology, and the like. There are several books already that give a good explanation of that. The focus of this book is on how to invest in crypto. The information here is not financial advice, but they are strategies worth considering.

In every crypto bull cycle, there is a constant trend that repeats itself: the rise of crypto gurus. And just in case you haven't gotten the point thus far, there are no crypto-investing gurus. I do not consider myself an expert. I am just someone quick with observation and able to find reasonable patterns.

There are so many unreasonable patterns in crypto. And many people will come to you explaining why a Chinese legislation is making the price of bitcoin surge. Those things are unreasonable patterns. And if you invest based on them, you will lose money.

The big lesson of this chapter is to stay away from the chatter of fake teachers. They may be good people with nice personalities, but don't let that dupe you into making a dumb investment. Most people lose money in crypto, not because of the volatility of bitcoin, but because they don't know what they are doing.

This is like someone coming to the football field wearing golfer's attire. You know very well that someone is going to get hurt. The game is not unfair, people just come in unprepared.

There are five basic signs that someone you're following for crypto advice might be a fake teacher. Again, I must add that they may not be intentionally teaching people wrongly, but you must be able to see the BS from afar and be discerning.

The first sign is being emotional over the current price of bitcoin. This is one of the ways to know a newbie who is pretending to be a legend. Legends laugh at everything. But newbies get excited. Excitement is a bad sign. It was okay to be excited in the very early days of crypto, such as 2010 and 2011. But after a decade, a true mentor is not excited about fluctuations in price.

The second sign is when you see them making social media posts like, "This changes everything." I'm sorry to burst your bubble, but nothing is going to change "everything" at this stage. This is just a way to make a news post sound more relevant than it is. No one who talks like that has enough in-depth understanding to teach others.

The third sign needs some background explanation. The crypto wave started in 2009 when bitcoin came onto the scene. Almost everyone active in the crypto space was busy with something before 2009. (In 2009, I was in university). While it is not okay to judge people by their pasts, I think it is important to know what a "crypto guru" was busy with before bitcoin.

Why is this important? It tells you a bit about why their approach to bitcoin is the way it is. Of course, it doesn't tell the entire story, but it gives a very important context to the story. I like to know what people are playing at. I like to know their gameplay. Even though the industry, commodities, and assets are different, the gameplay is often the same.

The core gameplay of most people never changes. They just adapt their gameplay to their new environment and circumstance.

So, if you find someone getting your attention about crypto, try to find out what the person was doing before crypto. This is not to judge, it is just for context.

The fourth sign you are dealing with a false mentor is when they harbor the idea of "I am right and everybody else is wrong." Crypto can make anyone look like a fool in this regard. Anyone expressing this mentality in the crypto industry is fake in some way. Real teachers know that they can be wrong and admit it.

One beautiful thing about crypto is that it has introduced a new concept of democracy. And it is the system where the best ideas win. Even if the idea is from a random kid in a basement, you will have to present a superior argument to dismiss the idea. This is why bitcoin is often called the people's money.

It is immature for anyone to make an assertion of absolutes with regards to crypto. Even the leading figures in the industry are finding new ideas every day. If you have spent over four active years in the crypto community, at one point you definitely had (at least) one idea which you assumed was an absolute that time has proved wrong. I have had a couple of them, and the ideas in this book are definitely not absolutes.

Only the immature speaks in absolutes.

The fifth sign of a fake teacher is their seasonality. If you only see them during the bull runs, that tells you everything you need to know. There is a famous bitcoin investor that is active on Twitter and also appears as a guest on CNBC. One thing I appreciate about him is that he shows up in all seasons. I have seen him show up in bull cycles. And I have seen him show up in bear cycles. Whether you agree with his analogy or not, his consistency deserves respect.

Don't believe the fancy excuses of "gurus" who become silent during the bear cycle. Yes, it is not a nice time to talk about crypto. But those who run away are definitely fake teachers.

It is okay to be an enthusiast and not a teacher. If you don't have the nerve to stand with bitcoin at $3,500, then you probably should not jump on the bandwagon at $60K.

Beware of fake teachers. And if you want to be a real teacher, I have one piece of advice:

Never underestimate how high bitcoin's price can go AND never underestimate how low bitcoin's price can go.

CHAPTER 17

Reading Charts Is Not for Trading

Unless you are a professional trader, reading charts is almost meaningless. When people start explaining their next trade based on charts, I can't hide the inevitable laughter.

Don't get me wrong; there are people who are good with charts and make a decent amount of money from that. But that is less than 97% of the people reading this book. And I do not advise you to go learn how to read charts because you want to trade crypto. The learning curve is long and full of tears. Every time you feel like you've understood how to read the charts, one faulty trade will humble you.

But there is something I use charts to do. I use them as part of the parameters to tell where we are in the crypto cycle. So, I don't merely check prices (when I have a reason to check), I also look at the chart to see where we are in the cycle.

There are four phases in the crypto cycle:

The first is the **bullish phase**. This is when prices are surging upwards every day and everybody is excited about the amount their crypto portfolio now displays.

The second is the **crash phase**. This is when prices start going down and everyone begins to panic. This is also when people are in denial about the impending bearish trend.

The third phase is the **pain phase**. Prices continue to gradually descend over a long period of time. This continues until price charts become almost flat (meaning that the changes in price become insignificant).

The fourth phase is the **confusion phase**. This is when the price charts display something like a horizontal zigzag. There are short significant gains and short significant losses. This is where the intellectual and fundamental arguments begin to gain mainstream attention again.

If you think you can play smart, then use this advanced playbook:

- Sell during the bullish phase
- Do nothing during the crash phase
- Buy during the pain phase
- Add your voice (support) to the arguments during the confusion phase

(But do know that you are responsible for the profits or losses you make using these tips. This is more risky than the strategy outlined in Chapter 1, hence greedy people who think they are smart will make losses.) This game plan is based on the past performance of crypto. It is not a surety of the future performance.

The bullish and pain phases are often long. They can take several months, depending on several factors. The crash phase is often short and emotional. The confusion phase can also take many weeks. But it is not as long as the bullish and pain phase.

If you don't look critically, you can mistake the phases for each other. You can mistake the confusion phase for the bullish phase. You can mistake the crash phase for the pain phase. And this is why I look at the charts. It is mainly to confirm my hunch about the current phase.

The first thing I look at is the one-month chart. My favorite view is the candlestick because I like having a visual of the volume of trades that are happening (which is a very important parameter). One month is long enough to give me the right perspective of the market and short enough to give me an overview of the current situation. I can only trust the green and red candles of the one-month price chart.

If I am still confused about the current phase, I check the six-month chart. What I look for is the sign that we have exited one phase and entered another.

The only reason I check the weekly or daily price chart is to check the trading volume. A trading volume that is decreasing on a consistent basis signifies that we are definitely not in a bullish phase. And if all other signs point to the fact that we are still in a bullish phase, it means an exit is close.

When I check the one-month chart, I look for two specific signs:

The first is lower highs. This means the highest points of the green candles are lower than the previous green candle highs. This means one thing in my opinion. The price is going to go lower.

The second is higher lows. This means that the bottoms of the red candles are higher than the previous red candle bottoms. In my opinion, this means that an uptrend trend has begun or is about to begin.

I don't check these to time the market. Timing the market is virtually impossible. I just do it to be aware of the current phase. There are other signs that come together to give a sort of confirmation about the current phase. Sometimes I miss a new phase by as much as four weeks. I'd rather wait for all the signs to point in confirmation before I make my move.

As I write these very words in early July 2021, the crypto market is between the crash phase and pain phase. I would wager that the market is still in the crash phase. People are still optimistic, so the pain has not really set in, or perhaps we are in the early stages of the pain. When a lot of well-known people start openly regretting buying bitcoin, that's a sure sign we are in the pain phase.

I don't read charts to trade. I watch charts to understand where we are in the crypto cycle. Reading charts to trade is like trying to know the temperature of water that is being heated by dipping your hand in every now and then. I don't do it and certainly would not recommend anyone else to do it. But if you have had the proper training for trading using charts, the world is your oyster.

CHAPTER 18

Air – Water – Fire – Bitcoin

There is still one problem yet to be properly addressed. And this is the question of how to designate crypto in your investment portfolio. This may not matter much to individuals, but it matters a lot for large investment bodies.

Asset allocation is a very important aspect of investment. And if you do not properly allocate crypto in your portfolio, you will make big investment errors that will lead to losses.

There are four major stages of the economic cycle:

- Rising economic growth
- Boom
- Declining economic growth
- Recession (which can turn into depression)

What you want to do is create a portfolio that performs well in all four stages of the economic cycle. Stocks perform well in the boom stage. Bonds perform fairly well when stocks do not. Commodities thrive based on the current situation of global trade and commerce. And cash is king when everybody is desperate to get money.

Bitcoin belongs to the cash aspect of the investment portfolio. Stocks, bonds, and commodities hedge themselves one way or another (when well arranged). But there is no hedge for cash. And cash gets devalued too.

So, bitcoin should be used in your portfolio as a hedge to your cash position. This is even more important because stocks, bonds, and commodities are still somewhat dependent on the value of local currency. And today, there are global events that cause all currencies to behave almost in the same way. Therefore, there is really no hedge.

If you diversify your cash position into USD, GBP, JPY, RUB, CNY, you are not really hedging. The events in recent years have proved that all currencies can all suffer the same fate at the same time. The only currency that has a different trajectory and behavior is bitcoin. Hence, bitcoin must take a reasonable position in your currency exposure.

So, in your portfolio you have:

- Stocks (such as Apple stock, tech index, energy ETF, etc.)
- Bonds (such as a 10-year bond, 30-year bond, 6-month bond, etc.)
- Commodities (such as gold, oil, silver, iron ore, wheat, etc.)
- Currencies (such as USD, CNY, RUB, GBP, BTC, etc.)

What about other cryptocurrencies aside from bitcoin? You have to class them differently. I would put them in the same bucket as an early-stage investment in a startup. If your investment group does not deal in early-stage startups, maybe you should not look at cryptocurrencies other than bitcoin.

If your investment group does not deal in early-stage startups but you still want to have a go at other cryptocurrencies, then you should create another division of your portfolio and call it "lottery." Then you can trade other cryptocurrencies from the lottery division.

The lottery division must not be more than 1% of your portfolio. Around 0.5% will be good. This is because you could lose everything you've invested and, more importantly, you don't understand how those financial instruments work. When you have been trading them for a while and you have a sense of how they work and perform, you can move these cryptocurrencies into more serious divisions and attach more funds to them.

The crypto industry is still young, hence caution is required when investing in it (especially if you manage billions). Now you know how to class crypto in your investment portfolio.

CHAPTER 19

Dogecoin Billionaires

I know someone who made $17K from trading dogecoin (in early 2021). He got in fast and got out early. And I also know someone who made $21. But he lost $258 first. This is one of the primary lessons of crypto that I had to learn by experience: never listen to half of any story.

I was speaking to a friend who was just trying his luck in trading. He said he turned $20 into $200 by trading. But when I probed him further, he told me that he later went from $200 to $0. There is a lot of danger in listening to half-stories.

In early 2021, I went into a Clubhouse room where people were talking about the possibility of dogecoin going to $1. And there were close to a thousand people in the room. I listened for a bit and was surprised at how much hope they had in dogecoin's rise. This is a cryptocurrency that does not have an active development team.

Dogecoin didn't even get to 70 cents. The price crashed with the rest of the crypto market a few weeks later. Some even had the notion they would be billionaires with dogecoin.

Dogecoin has never made anyone a billionaire. And I doubt if it ever will. Can you make a decent profit from trading dogecoin? Emphatically YES! Can you also lose all your money? Definitely YES! This is why you need a strategy. Without a strategy, you are just gambling.

Why did one friend make $17K from dogecoin and another lost $237? Timing. When you are trading altcoins, you have to think about the timing a lot. If you hear about a cryptocurrency trading play from someone who heard it from someone, you are already late to the party.

I was having a conversation about crypto trading with an old colleague and friend. He is pretty sharp with trading. So I asked him if he has ever made money from mainnet launch trades. His answer was no. He lost money on every single one.

Mainnet launch trades were quite common in 2018. This is where several cryptocurrencies that raised money using the ethereum platform migrated people into their own platform and left the ethereum ecosystem. During the few hours of the mainnet launch, there is always a high level of trading activity that makes smart players a lot of money. I always knew it was a trap for casual traders and so I stayed away. But I was always curious.

My friend confirmed my suspicion. He lost every trade he made on mainnet launch trading. And this reminds me of the best-kept secret in crypto: people lose money a lot (but they rarely talk about it). Hence, you should have a strategy. Please, don't believe you are a genius because your first two trades made money.

Elon Musk is not a dogecoin billionaire. He was a billionaire before dogecoin. And I doubt if he has any significant amount of money in dogecoin. Yes, he may have moved money in and out of dogecoin. But I doubt if he has any amount of money in dogecoin for the long-term. Even though he is hilarious on Twitter, he is still one very smart guy.

The idea that Elon Musk is left holding the bag (that is, the no-activity cryptocurrencies no one else wants to buy) is hilarious. My guess is that if he ever went in, he got out long before the party was over.

Too many people build castles in the air. Trading without a strategy is gambling. And the thing about gambling is that over a long period of time your losses outweigh your gains, no matter how good you are. And if you know nothing about taxes to boot, you lose money on all fronts.

The only billionaires in crypto are builders and people who were billionaires (or close to billionaires) before crypto. People who set up funds and make massive investments in promising crypto projects can also grow to become billionaires. But the idea that you will trade bitcoin, dogecoin, dash, monero, etc., to become a billionaire is laughable.

I am aware people throw the word "billionaire" around just to trigger emotions, when really they would be happy with just a few thousands bucks. But that often gives them the confidence to throw away their money on dumb trades.

Another thing you should be wary of is crypto groups. Never, ever trust anything you hear in a group designed to shill crypto. (To shill means to only praise a certain crypto with the intention of causing other people to want to buy it). There are lots of crypto groups across the internet: on Facebook, WhatsApp, Telegram, etc.

Nobody is doing research for you. Never trust the research someone else has done and you don't really understand. Everybody is there for their own interest and theirs alone. If you hang around too much with shills, you will grow greedy.

Something interesting happened in a Telegram group sometime ago. A guy pretending to be a noob shared a screenshot of his crypto wallet details, exposing his private keys. Exposing his private keys meant that anyone who saw them could access his wallet and take what he had. It was an ether wallet that had a significant number of ethereum tokens (altcoins built on the ethereum platform). The cash value of what he had was in thousands of dollars. But there was a problem.

He had no ether to pay as gas fees to conduct any transaction. Therefore, to move any token from the account, you would have to send some ether into the wallet and then conduct the transaction. It was a no-brainer.

Several people in the group tried to steal the tokens from the wallet (since the private keys were obvious). So, they all began by sending some ether to the wallet. And now, this is the funny part.

The guy who owned the wallet had already written a script (or code) that automatically transferred any ether sent to that wallet into another wallet. So, everyone who tried to steal the tokens by sending some ether to the wallet lost their ether and still couldn't access the tokens. That is how one "honest" guy stole from people who had the intention of stealing from him.

But here is my point. A lot of people in the group made the attempt to steal the tokens. Finally, they had to applaud the genius of the guy who had shared his private keys. The lesson here is that nobody has your interest at heart. Everybody has their own interest. You cannot be sucked in by analyzing opportunities and potential in crypto. You need to have a strategy.

And one more thing. If you want to be a billionaire, build an amazing company or corporation. Don't trade crypto.

CHAPTER 20

Go Long or Go Home

There are two important timelines in crypto: 30 days and 4 years. From 2009 to 2021, if you hold onto bitcoin for any four-year period, the value grows (despite the volatility). Yes, past performance doesn't translate to future performance. But that has been a good historical metric.

Therefore, if you are going to be forced to sell in less than four years, maybe you shouldn't put that much investment in bitcoin. The strategy in Chapter 1 can lead to you selling at a profit in less than four years. In most cases, it will. But you must be prepared to wait for as long as four years before cashing out.

If you are not greedy, the timeline that should be on your mind for your bitcoin investment is four years. However, for other cryptocurrencies, there is a slightly different timeline.

Just as it has been discussed earlier, you should get out in 30 days if you are just merely trading in crypto. If you are involved in something that will be a big deal in the future, then you can hold on for the long-term. But if you just want to buy or sell for some profits, the recommended benchmark is 30 days.

If you are at a loss for the entire 30 days, just take what is left of your capital and leave. This is because it most likely won't get better. If you can afford to leave the money there for 1,000 years, go ahead and do so. But just because you wait for 1,000 years doesn't mean you will make profits. If you change your mind and decide to sell later, you will probably sell at an even greater loss.

If you are a fundamental analysis person and you believe in the future of crypto, with bitcoin becoming a globally recognized store of value and decentralized finance (DeFi) becoming mainstream, you can bet on that. But you must know that your bet is a gamble and not an investment.

You don't make investments based on the future. You make investments based on strategies. You are not trying to predict the future. Instead, you are trying to make profits. You can be right about the future and your gamble will still turn out wrong. There are so many ways things can turn out.

This is why it is better to have a sound strategy and stick to it. Don't let anybody tempt you to bet on your philosophy. And, if you do, make sure you're only betting an insignificant amount.

Generally, people would say "go long" with regards to your investment position. But here, I would advise you to go long with regards to your strategy. Do not deviate unless there are significant changes in the crypto industry that causes cryptocurrencies to perform differently from how they do currently. Don't let anyone sweet-talk you out of your strategy or discourage you from it.

My reason for stressing this is that you will be tempted to deviate. This is especially if you love listening to pundits. Pundits will lead you astray. Their job is to get you emotionally triggered about something. The moment you become emotionally triggered about any cryptocurrency, you are in a position to start making mistakes. I wouldn't add this chapter if the temptation was not real.

If you are not emotionally balanced enough to go long on your strategy, just go home. Do something with your money that is more in tune with your character.

You don't need to have an in-depth understanding of cryptocurrencies before you make quality investments. You just need to have a solid strategy that you are in tune with and then stick to that strategy.

Sometimes, the less you know, the better. If you have read this book without skipping any part, you know enough to invest profitably in crypto. More knowledge will likely lead you into something that will get you to invest with your emotions.

The problem of investing with your emotions is that you think you are a god the first time you make huge money. And that sets you up for a big loss later.

There is another thing worth mentioning here. When you hear a crypto-trading tip from a friend that you know is not neck-deep into crypto, it is already too late to jump on the trade. When your friend who works in the travel industry tells you about a hot crypto tip, it is already late. If you go in based on such advice, I would wager that 95% of the time you will get burned.

Only believe tips from people that you know who are close to the action. And just because you believe a tip doesn't mean you should jump on it. Personally, I don't follow tips. I stick to my strategy. I would encourage you to do the same, but some just wouldn't agree. So if you are going to be following tips, they must be from people who are very knowledgeable about crypto.

You must have at least one person to confirm the tips that reach you if you are going to be acting on them. When I respond to people who ask me to confirm a tip they've received, I don't tell them what to do (even though that is what they all want). Most don't want to take responsibility for their actions. They just want to be able to say, "You told me to do it."

My response instead is to give them options. In most cases, I show them the consequences in all directions. And they decide which consequence they are okay with. If you are in the position to confirm tips, people will want you to make decisions for them. Make sure you stay away from that. It can create massive problems legally, socially, and emotionally.

The summary of this chapter is to go long on your strategy. That is how to win.

CHAPTER 21

Crypto Funds and Cloud Mining Deals

I have invested in crypto funds. In fact, I once ran a (trial, unofficial) crypto fund. I have also put my money in cloud mining deals. So, I share these insights with you because I have been there, and I doubt if anything about them has changed.

I don't boast of having technical knowledge about these things. In fact, to most technical people, I am a novice. But when it comes to the investing part, I know my jam. I know my game. This book is not written to be relevant for a particular time period. It was written to stand the test of time and be a guide for non-greedy crypto investors for decades, except and unless a "Nexus" event happens.

When you put your money in a bitcoin fund, you are not buying bitcoin. You are putting your money in an investment vehicle that has bitcoin. If they fail to deliver on their promise, you can't take their bitcoin away from them as payment.

If your money is in a bitcoin fund, you are betting on the people running the fund knowing what they are doing. (In the next chapter, I will share questions you should ask a crypto investor or fund manager to get a sense of whether they really know what they are doing.)

The bitcoin fund is not a good or bad decision. It all depends on the results you get. If you don't want to throw your money away, you must ensure that the fund managers know what they are doing. Personally, I see no sense in this unless you have a very large amount of money. And if you have that, you should be able to interview the fund managers. If you can't interview them for yourself, then you should maybe just let go of the idea. If the fund managers are hard to reach when they want your money, think about how hard it will be to reach them when you want your money back.

If it is a technological platform, that is better. But if you are investing in a fund and you have no rights to the bitcoins they own, know the game you are playing and the risks associated with that game.

Funds that trade multiple cryptocurrencies are much crazier. Unless you have a sure way of holding them accountable, stay away. And the legal system of your country doesn't qualify as a sure way of holding them accountable. Never bank on that; it should be a last resort only. When you have to look to the legal system for help, you have already lost. Even if you regain the money, you will have wasted a lot of time.

There are other kinds of funds, though. These are funds that invest in projects that are building the crypto industry. These kinds of funds make a lot of sense from an investing perspective. They are like Venture Capital firms. But instead of focusing on startups, they focus on projects that are developing the crypto ecosystem.

Just like startups, not every one of these projects works. In fact, it often takes a long time before the profitable model of the crypto project becomes clear. As such, investing in a fund that is building the crypto industry is a game of chance and numbers. Most people do it because of their belief in the crypto industry, not because they assume they will make profits.

A better step than this is to create your own fund to invest in growing the crypto industry (if you really believe in it that much). But my suggestion to you if this is the case is that you find crypto investment firms that are already doing this. There are several of them. Make a list of 12 firms and go speak with the leaders of those firms. They will give you more perspective into the intricate details of how such funds function. Don't expect them to give you their playbook, though.

You can also create your own fund to trade bitcoin and other cryptocurrencies while managing other people's money. I did a trial version of this when my understanding of crypto was still below par. And I thank God for the clauses in the contract that I made everyone sign. I drew up a couple of scenarios which included a worst-case scenario. And the worst-case scenario would still be profitable for my clients. And in the end, the worst-case scenario was what happened.

I ran the crypto fund for the experience and I enjoyed it. It was a good learning curve. But I'm not sure I would want to do that again. Managing your own money is one thing. Managing other people's money is a whole different ball game. The pressure is different.

If you are going to manage other people's money:

- Set their expectations right;
- Be transparent about the different scenarios that can happen;
- Be accountable;
- Be responsible (get ahead of rumors);
- Draft a contract that will cater for any anomaly;
- Don't be greedy.

You will have some people who will be a pain in your butt. You must have a clause in the contract that explains how to resolve that situation. You must have a system for kicking those people out. There will be people who will misbehave. If they know they can be kicked out, the tendency to misbehave will be less.

Now to cloud mining. Most cryptocurrencies are mined (with a few exceptions, based on how they are designed to function). Crypto mining does not mean there are large earth machines drilling deep into a piece of land or blowing up a hill. The mining operation is done by computers.

The raw value of bitcoin is actually measured in the computing power it takes to mine it. And the computing power takes a lot of electrical energy. So, those who say bitcoin has no intrinsic value are wrong. This is because if I expend electrical energy (which I got by paying money) to get bitcoin, then the intrinsic value of bitcoin is (at least) the value of the energy I used to get it.

In the early days, bitcoin mining was a very profitable venture. But with time and public adoption, it became more difficult. Individuals used to be able to mine bitcoin on their own computers. But as the difficulty increased, special computing systems were required. And as the difficulty kept increasing, people had to set up special mines with tons of computing power. Also, they had to find cost-effective ways of generating the energy required.

The computing machines used to get very hot during the mining process, hence there is a need for a cooling system. As a result, mining crypto became an industrial venture. And it still is.

But at the start, many entrepreneurs who wanted to start a mining farm (as it is fondly called) did not have all the funds required. Seeing that they couldn't get money from banks and there was a significant upside to their venture (based on how many bitcoins they foresaw making), they decided to go into crowdfunding. And it worked.

People who wanted to mine but who didn't want to deal with managing computing machines saw the "mining farms" as an opportunity. They (me included) jumped on the opportunity. This was called cloud mining. The entrepreneurs mined from their farms and then sent us crypto coins based on how much we invested in their mining farms.

I invested in three major cloud mining operations around 2017 and 2018. One was an outright scam. That money is gone. The last I heard, the case is still in some European court. The hope that was dashed was more painful than the money I had invested. So, I just gave up on it. Interestingly, the scam had the most amazing idea of all the cloud mining operations; they were going to use a certain mobile technique to create the most profitable bitcoin farm.

The second mining farm delivered for a while. But when they needed more money, they launched another round of crowdfunding. They packaged this as an ICO. And then, I knew that some gimmick was going to happen. Long story short, they sort of abandoned (financially) those who participated in the crowdfunding. Both the first round and the second one. They continued communication though. They had underestimated the crypto bear market. So, I guess they made serious losses too.

The third mining farm was more sturdy. They kept going until bitcoin dipped below a certain threshold (which was in the contract we had all signed). They said they would stop paying out if bitcoin dipped below that threshold. This was because they spent dollars to maintain the business, but they generated revenue in bitcoin. So at a certain exchange rate, the mining farm was just not profitable anymore.

They asked us to invest more money if we wanted to continue. I didn't. And when the price of bitcoin bounced back, they didn't reactivate the mining contract. But they stayed true with those who reinvested with them, and their mining farm still exists as of writing.

The lesson I have learned from these three investments are:

- Never underestimate the crypto bear market;
- Always read the fine print of every contract;
- Cloud mining is not automatic passive income;
- Scams are often beautiful projects;
- A business venture is as good as the entrepreneur in charge.

Today, I would not invest in cloud mining for two reasons:

1. Those in charge will underestimate the crypto bear market; and
2. The mining difficulty is much higher now (and the difficulty will keep increasing).

There is a new fad with crypto passive income. And this is staking. You give your bitcoins to people to trade on your behalf and they pay you interests on their gains. Or you give your bitcoins up and loans are issued out based on them, and you get a piece of the interest on those loans. Or you stake your bitcoins as collateral and use it to take out a loan in dollars (or your local currency). There are several other variants of this.

The important thing here is to read the fine print. What happens during a crypto bear market? What happens when the loan you got in dollars is now greater than the bitcoin you staked? What happens if you want to sell? All these contingencies will be accounted for in the terms and conditions of staking your bitcoins.

This all boils down to the fact that you can lose your bitcoins in a bear market (at exactly the wrong time to sell). Always remember never to underestimate the crypto bear market. The bear often gets so bad that failsafe clauses get triggered in many contracts. This has happened several times already. And it will almost undoubtedly happen again.

This is not financial advice. This is my perspective and experience; you are responsible for your own decisions.

CHAPTER 22

8 Questions for a Crypto Fund Manager

The questions below are to help you determine whether the fund manager you are talking to deserves to manage your money. The first thing you must understand here is that past performance is not an indication of future performance. Yet, most people judge fund managers by their track record.

A track record is good, but you don't want a fund manager that is lucky or a fund manager that is about to make a mistake. You want one that has a sustainable understanding of crypto investing. There are no hard and fast answers here for these questions. But you can tell someone who knows their stuff based on how they respond.

QUESTION 1: ARE BITCOIN AND ALL OTHER CRYPTOCURRENCIES THE SAME?

A fund manager that considers all cryptocurrencies the same (from an investment standpoint) is an accident waiting to happen. This question will clarify that the manager is not merely day trading as opposed to having a long-term strategy. If your fund manager doesn't agree that there is a distinction here, all they are going to do is day trade your money. If that is what you want, fine. But accidents do happen with day trading, even when it is high-frequency trading by algorithms.

The lifespan of cryptocurrency is not long enough to have a trading algorithm that perfectly understands it. Yes, there can be good algorithms, but until the crypto industry is over 40 years old, trading algorithms are largely experimental.

QUESTION 2: HOW DO YOU CLASSIFY CRYPTOCURRENCIES IN YOUR PORTFOLIO? SECURITIES? COMMODITIES? PROPERTY? CURRENCY?

As of writing, the legal systems around the world are trending towards looking at crypto as property. And that is good. But fund managers look at it in many different ways, which determines their strategy. If any of them say they view it as property too, they are (most likely) lying. If they are not lying, then they don't really know what they are doing.

QUESTION 3: WHAT HAPPENS WHEN THE PRICE OF BITCOIN CRASHES?

Your fund manager must at least have a strategy or contingency for that. If you feel that their measures to deal with a price crash are too extreme, then you should stay away. If they only know how to make money when the price is going up, then they are speculators and not investors.

QUESTION 4: IF SOMEONE WANTS TO TAKE MONEY OUT, WHAT IS THE PROCEDURE?

Most people only think about putting money in and watching it grow. Most people don't think about taking money out. Of course, the fund managers never want you to take your money out. But you must know the procedure to do that. It separates those who know what they are doing from those who don't.

The procedure must not be too easy and it must not be too hard. (But it should be a bit hard if they know what they are doing.) The procedure should take a number of weeks, especially if the funds are very large. Anyone that is willing to shake the market because a client needs their money back is an amateur.

QUESTION 5: HOW DO YOU KEEP YOUR CRYPTOCURRENCIES?

Safeguarding cryptocurrencies is very important. Yes, cryptocurrencies get stolen. They get lost. People who know the private keys can go into a coma. All kinds of complications can happen. A fund that doesn't have a proper system to safeguard its cryptocurrencies will have problems soon enough.

There is a hidden question here too. Depending on how they answer, you will find out whether they really have cryptocurrencies of their own. If all they have is bitcoin ETFs, then that is not a crypto fund.

QUESTION 6: HOW LONG HAVE YOU BEEN DOING THIS?

There was nothing like crypto funds in 2010. Those were the very early days. I doubt if there were any active funds in 2015/2016.

By 2017, there were some bold fund managers jumping on the idea of crypto funds. My experimental fund (with money from friends, family, and my own savings) was in 2017/2018.

The idea here is to know if they are lying to you. Anyone who will lie to you to take your money will get greedy. And that greed will lead to losses.

QUESTION 7: ARE YOU DIVERSIFIED?

"Yes" or "No" is irrelevant here. What you are looking for here is one word. And that word is "cash." You want managers who recognize the need to have a cash position relative to their crypto holdings.

QUESTION 8: ARE YOU BETTING ON THE FUTURE POTENTIAL OF ANY CRYPTOCURRENCY?

There are money managers and there are crypto venture-capital firms. The crypto venture-capital firms have their place as they invest in building and developing the crypto industry. However, it is those who are fixated on managing money who win.

Smart money managers put a portion into firms that fund the development of the crypto industry. However, if you are not investing to develop the crypto industry, then don't sink your money into funds that are doing only that. Entrust your money to people that understand how to grow money steadily. Don't get carried away by the projections of people who are betting on a certain kind of future for a particular crypto project.

There are a few more questions to ask that concern the following areas: legal, compliance, asset allocation, failsafe strategy, dispute resolution, tax & accounting, and leadership. But they have to be tailored questions, asked in such a way so as to produce honest answers.

There is no set way to ask those questions, but you must find some way to get honest answers.

A fund manager that gives excellent to satisfactory answers to six out of the first eight questions is very likely to be good. But you must always do your homework and research before you decide. Hiring a private investigator is not a bad idea. Everyone looks good when they are asking for money. You can tell true investors and fund managers when others are failing (and falling) and they keep standing in the midst of the chaos.

CHAPTER 23

Crypto's Worst Enemy

Yes, crypto has enemies. Some are self-appointed enemies who gloat every time the price of crypto drops. Some are just plain haters. Some have said, "It is killing babies." (Incidentally, I still don't understand the correlation).

Others have said the energy consumption by bitcoin miners is not good for the environment. (I wonder what technology doesn't.) Apparently, some environmentalists like to guilt-trip anything new that uses a lot of energy. But they are not crypto's worst enemy. They are not even enemies; they are just haters.

But crypto has a real enemy. And the worst enemy of crypto is the central bank. In America, this is known as the Federal Reserve Bank of America. In England, this is known as the Bank of England. In the rest of Europe, this is known as the European Central Bank. In China, this is known as the People's Bank of China. In Japan, this is known as the Bank of Japan. (And so on.) And all these central banks collaborate with each other one way or another. And whether you like them or hate them, they control the financial reality of the world to a very large extent.

Central banks can ban the trading of crypto on the official channels of the country in which they have jurisdiction. However, that is no threat. Even big countries like China have done that to bitcoin, and bitcoin is still going strong. So, the problem is not the ban.

The real problem is monetary and fiscal policy. For example, bitcoin is priced in US dollars. But the Federal Reserve controls the flow of US dollars. Hence, they can encourage a massive buy or sell-off by large buyers (called whales) through policy.

The central bank does not only control the flow of money, they control economic behavior to a very large extent. Many financial regulations are rooted in the recommendations of the central bank. The central bank is more powerful than the government in this context. This is because the government does not control the central bank, but the central bank can steer (or, in some cases, manipulate) the government.

Now, the US dollar (or any other fiat currency) is not the enemy. The local currencies help give a price to crypto and encourage people to use it any way they want. So, that is not the problem here. The problem is that if the central banks want institutions who hold bitcoin in large volume to dump it, they can make that happen. They may not do it directly. In fact, they may not mention bitcoin or crypto at all.

They can just say that institutions with a high cash balance sheet with no digital assets can access a certain privilege. Yes, some institutions will refuse to let go of their digital assets, but most will gladly trade theirs off. It is just a policy, the central bank will argue. And they will defend that policy to the public in a glamorous way on mainstream media. And the media will bring in economists from prestigious schools to back up the narrative.

That cannot kill bitcoin. It won't make bitcoin go to zero. But it can certainly crash the price of bitcoin. This power of the central bank isn't going to disappear anytime soon. In other words, the position of the central bank on crypto is more important than the position of the government on crypto. In fact, in every country where crypto was banned, if you dig deep you will discover that the suggestion came from the central bank. If it didn't, the central bank must at least have been consulted before such policies were announced. The government has too many things to deal with for them to be preoccupied with crypto.

This is also a double-edged sword. The greatest threat to the central banking system is crypto. Some have said it is DeFi (more specifically). But here is my point. The central bank holds the power to create money. Crypto is living proof that anybody can create money and the public will accept it. This is why the government killed the attempts by top companies such as Facebook and Telegram to venture into crypto (and create their own money).

There is a certain ideology around creating a cryptocurrency that makes it impossible for certain players. Public acceptance is a big deal. For example, the central bank might want to create their own cryptocurrency, but how would the public respond? I think that would be a good thing though. It would be fun to watch a central bank's cryptocurrency compete with bitcoin for supremacy.

Why is this information about central banks here? Well, there is a saying, "Keep your friends close, and your enemies closer." If you are going to invest massively in crypto, you'll have to keep crypto's worst enemy very close. It will be amazing if it ever gets to the point where crypto influencers can influence the central bank. As of writing, this is still a pipe dream. But it is a concept worth pursuing.

If you are putting billions into crypto, make friends with the central bank. Don't ask me how. If you can't make friends with the central bank, then keep them very close. It will be so much fun to get them to fully dance to the tune of crypto and not be an enemy anymore.

However, don't get your guard down. Even when they seem to be dancing to the tune of crypto, you should never get too comfortable. The central bank has been in the game far, far, far longer than crypto. They are way better at the game, honestly. So, if it seems crypto is winning and the central bank is bleeding out, stay sharp and keep your eyes peeled. They are pros at this game.

The worst enemy of crypto is the central bank. If you are investing multiple millions and billions into crypto, keep your friends close and your enemies closer.

CHAPTER 24

A Moral Compass

An important activity in the crypto world is "shilling." If you don't understand the crypto jargon, it means to talk about something (mostly, something you have) in a way that causes others to think highly of it. In the crypto world, the players who are neck-deep into a crypto project spend a lot of time shilling it.

They are trying to create a perception of value to drive the project forward. In most cases, the effort is geared towards the price going higher. And there are several variants of this.

There are fundamental shills. These are shills that are based on the problem a project solves or the way it works. The aim of this is to get people to appreciate the significance of the project. This is very common and in most cases the person shilling the cryptocurrency genuinely believes in the project.

Then there are pricing shills. These are shills that emphasize the fact that a particular cryptocurrency is undervalued at its current price. And this is where the dishonesty lies. You cannot say that a cryptocurrency is undervalued at any price. I had to learn this by experience.

In 2018, I watched the price of bitcoin go significantly lower than the cost of mining bitcoin. I used to think that couldn't happen. But it did. At that stage, some would argue that the price of bitcoin was undervalued. But it wasn't. The price is the price. There is no undervalue or overvalue price. This is because the price is determined by market forces. The price is always the current settlement between those who want to buy and those who want to sell.

Think about this. If people are selling bitcoin en masse and very few are interested in buying, bitcoin is not undervalued. Instead, the price is down. Future price projections are like castles in the air. If you are particular about where bitcoin's price is going next, you lose. You can only understand where the price is and where it was.

You can understand bitcoin's phases, but you shouldn't try to understand price targets. For 99% of people, price target projection is going to result in losses. And for those who think they are in the 1%, if your information is based on a tweet or a YouTube video, I will be on a couch somewhere getting ready to laugh at you.

There is also the celebrity shill. A lot of crypto dudes jump on newsworthy information like this. You hear things like, "Michael Jackson is back from the dead and the first thing he did was to buy this crypto coin. What does he know that you don't?"

Okay. Here is a more realistic one, "Every time Elon Musk tweets about dogecoin, it goes up in price. Now that he's going live on this hit TV show, dogecoin is going to the moon." It always ends in tears. And I have seen many variants of this through the years.

Here is another one, "Binance is going to add this new crypto coin. CZ has even tweeted about it. Do you know how many crypto traders are on Binance? Do you have any idea how many people listen to CZ?" It will end in tears. Even if you are the smartest crypto trader, algorithms will trade faster.

Here is another one: "Steve Wozniak is backing this new cryptocurrency that is building the iOS of Web 3.0. The price has already surged 200% from last week." The interesting thing is that the information might be true. But that doesn't mean the crypto's price can't still crash. This kind of shill happens during the bull cycle.

Understand this: crypto does not need a reason for the price to crash. Yes, people make up reasons after it happens. But in many cases, they just aren't accurate. This is the only reason the price goes down; more people are willing to sell, very few are willing to buy. You don't need any other explanation.

And this leads to the concluding thought of this book. If you work on a crypto project or you are a highly respected voice in the crypto space, pay attention to what you say. You can shill, but please shill responsibly.

Crypto doesn't have strong laws or regulations with regards to tips and trades. And I hope it stays that way. But the industry has to hold itself to a high moral standard if it intends to stay out of the reach of the kinds of laws that regulate Wall Street. And this means being objective enough that information shared does not cause a pump-and-dump event.

Pump-and-dump schemes weaken the crypto industry. If your information causes a pump (whether you intend it to or not), stay away from anything that will suggest a dump (at least, for a good number of weeks). Let the market find its natural flow.

I can stand crypto-haters and no-coiners. I can stand cyberpunks and crypto-believers. Those I can't stand are people who are believers one minute and haters the next. You should never listen to anything people like that say. That is because their loyalty can be bought (intentionally or unintentionally) into a pump-and-dump scheme.

I do not consider myself a crypto-believer. I am an investing strategist. And this book is designed to help you become a better crypto investor.

I rest my case.

EPILOGUE

Now that your curiosity has been satisfied about the contents of this book, I will implore you to go read Chapter 1 again. That is the most sustainable strategy that anybody can follow.

I will also remind you at this point that trading crypto is not the same thing as making money. You can see it as keeping money, saving money, preserving money, or investing money. But you make money from whatever your job or business is, and then you preserve some of it in crypto. This is the simplest way I have seen that anyone can go about it.

If you see yourself as a professional trader, then don't ignore the warnings and signs shared all across this book. If you manage huge funds, pay attention to the areas that pertain to you. In my opinion, the less emotional you are about crypto, the more you can really grow your money.

Each time you catch yourself being greedy, that is a good time to read this book (or part of this book) again. Hopefully, my attempts to poke fun at the moves of greedy people will serve as a warning.

If you are in a position where a lot of people listen to what you have to say on crypto, be careful with your shills. Feel free to be funny. But don't cause crypto to lose credibility because of irresponsible communications. I like the crypto industry. There is nothing like it. And I believe it is here to stay. And I want it to keep increasing in its credibility without the prying eyes of regulators and lawmakers.

Now that this book is in your hands, I hope to never again have to answer basic, fundamental questions about buying bitcoin and other cryptocurrencies. I hope to have more high-level discussions on investing in crypto, in private and with people that matter (and only publicly when it is highly required).

I hope you take what you have learned from this book and use it to make successful investments. Cheers.

www.ingramcontent.com/pod-product-compliance
Ingram Content Group UK Ltd.
Pitfield, Milton Keynes, MK11 3LW, UK
UKHW021523300726
14060UKWH00016B/735/J

9 780578 976730